Governor William Bradford's Letter Book

Reprinted from The Mayflower Descendant

By William Bradford

PANTIANOS
CLASSICS

Published by Pantianos Classics

ISBN-13: 978-1-78987-555-3

First published in 1906

Contents

Introductory Note

Governor Bradford's Letter Book is so little known it has been decided to reprint it in this magazine and make it accessible to all. Unfortunately the fragment of the original manuscript rescued by Mr. Clarke cannot now be found, and the text printed in the "Collections of the Massachusetts Historical Society," Volume III (1794), pages 27 to 76 inclusive, has been followed. From the first volume of the "Proceedings" of the same society we also reprint in full the account of the receipt of the manuscript, and notes regarding it.

[Proceedings, Vol. I, pp. 51, 52]
At a meeting of the Historical Society, on Tuesday, the thirtieth day of July, 1793, at Winthrop's or Governor's Island.............
The following donations were received: —
For the Library: — Fragment of a MS. Letter-book of Governor Bradford, of Plymouth, from 1624 to 1630, found in a grocer's shop in Halifax, Nova Scotia. From James Clarke, Esq., of Halifax.

This fragment of Governor Bradford's Letter-book was printed in Vol. III. of the Collections, making fifty pages. It appears from a note at the beginning of the printed text that the MS. of the part preserved began with "page 339, the preceding pages wanting," and covered the years 1624—1630. This shows that what was recovered was but a small part of what was lost; while it is probable that the collection originally contained also letters of a later date than 1630. Governor Bradford's History dosed with the year 1646, and the letters which he had preserved to illustrate that part of the narrative, from 1630 to its conclusion, may have been included in his Letter-book, as well as those used in the earlier portion. The fragment recovered may have been one volume of a series continuously paged. The fortunate recovery of Governor Bradford's History, some sixty years after Mr. James Clarke rescued this fragment from a grocer's shop in Halifax, happily supplies to a certain extent the place of the Letter-book; for, while the author did not copy into his History all these letters, we may well suppose him, judging from the use he made of those preserved, to have used the most valuable part of them.

The finding of this manuscript in Halifax naturally suggests the thought that it left Boston at the time of the "evacuation," in March, 1776; and, it being well known that the British soldiers during the occupation of Boston had free access to the Historical Library of books and manuscripts of the Rev. Thomas Prince, kept in a room in the tower of the Old South Meeting-house, that it was taken from that collection. This is not improbable. There may be no positive evidence that Prince's Library then contained this Letter-book, yet we know that it was once in Prince's possession. For, besides the manuscripts of Bradford, which he mentions, in the preface to his Chronological History, as having had an "opportunity to search," — namely, "Bradford's History of Plymouth People and Colony," in folio, and "A Register of Governor Bradford's, in his own hand, recording some of the first deaths, marriages, and punishments at Plymouth, with three other miscellaneous volumes of his," in octavo, — he several times refers, in his notes on the margin of Bradford's manuscript History, to "Governor Bradford's Collection of Letters." See pp. 47, 61, 64, and 71 of the printed volume. [1]

The following is the letter of Mr. Clarke which accompanied the manuscript:

"Halifax, May 28, 1793.

"Sir, — The enclosed ancient manuscript I found some years ago in a grocer's shop in this town, of whom I obtained it with a view of saving what remained from destruction. I lament extremely that a page has been torn out; and it gives me pleasure that I now have an opportunity of placing it in your hands, — a freedom I am induced to take from your advertisement of the first of November, 1792, and from a persuasion that it may contribute in some measure to the important objects of your Society, and I could wish I might otherwise be serviceable.

"I am, respectfully. Sir, your most obedient humble servant,

"James Clarke.

"The Rev. Jeremy Belknap."

Where the writer speaks of a *page* being torn out, he probably means that one *leaf* had been torn out of the volume. Bradford may have written on one side only of the leaf in copying his letters, as he generally did in writing his History, so that one leaf would represent one page of writing. — Eds.

[1] Edition of 1856.

Governor Bradford's Letter Book

[Page 339 — the preceding pages wanting.]

To our beloved and right well esteemed friend Mr. William Bradford Governour these, but inscribed thus:

To our beloved friends Mr. William Bradford, Mr. Isaac Allerton, Mr. Edward Winslow, and the rest whom, they think fit to acquaint therewith.

Two things (beloved friends) we have endeavoured to effect, touching Plymouth plantation, first, that the planters there might live comfortably and contentedly. 2d that some returns might be made hither for the satisfying and encouragement of the adventurers, but to neither of these two can we yet attain. Nay, if it be as some of them report which returned in the Catherine, it is almost impossible to hope for it, since, by their sayings, the slothfulness of one part of you, and the weakness of the other part, is such, that nothing can go well forward. And although we do not wholly credit these reports, yet surely, either the country is not good where you are, for habitation; or else there is something amiss amongst you; and we much fear the willing are too weak and the strong too idle. And because we will not stand upon the number of the objections made by them against you; we have sent them here enclosed, that you may see them and answer them. *(These are those which are inserted and answered before in this book; namely, before Liford's letters y where those letters should also have been placed, but they came not then to hand and I thought better to put them in, than to omit them.)*

As for such as will needs be upon their particulars now that they are gotten over, you must be sure to make such covenants with them, as that first or last the company be satisfied for all their charge. Neither must you proceed to these agreements and consultations with many at once, otherwise how easy might *they* make a lead in rebellion, which have so long done it in cheating and idleness.

Touching Mr. Weston, his disturbing of you about that £100 taken up for Mr. Brewer, except we conclude with Solomon that oppression maketh a wise man mad, we cannot but wonder at it, seeing under his own hand, it is apparently and particularly expressed, summed up and sold with the rest of his adventures, so as no sober man can possibly question it. 2dly, had it not been sold, Mr. Brewer might well have had it, to pay himself part of a debt which Mr. Weston oweth him for commodities sold to him, which he saith amounteth to above £100, as he can prove by good testimony. 3dly, if it had not been apparently sold, Mr. Beuchamp who is of the company also, unto whom he oweth a great deal more, had long ago attached it (as he did other's 16ths) and so he could not have demanded it, either of you or us.

And if he will not believe our testimony here about, who shall believe his, either in this, or any other matters. It is a dangerous case when a man groweth naught in prosperity, and worse in adversity, and what can the end of all this be, but more and more misery. And for conclusion with him, you may shew him what we have wrote about him, and if that satisfy him not, but that he shall still follow his mad and malicious practices against you, warn him out of your precincts, and let it be upon his peril to set foot thereon; it being indeed no reason that a whole plantation should be disturbed or indamaged by the frantic humours of any one man whatsoever.

Now further for yourselves; as the power of government is fallen upon you, both by lot and desert (as we are persuaded) so your troubles and cares have been so much the more hitherto; and we would not have you think of easing yourselves till you have either made things better, or ended your warfare; for it is best that the world afford us these crosses lest we should forget the meditation of heaven.

And we pray you all even look to yourselves, and your ways; that there be not amongst you some cause or occasion of these evil men's insultings and bravery upon you, as they do, that we charge you with nothing, but are ready to make your just defence at all times against opposites; yet let it not offend you, that we wish you to look to yourselves, as first that you walk close with God, being fervent and frequent in prayer, instruction and doctrine, both openly and privately. 2dly, that you instruct and bring up your young ones in the knowledge and fear of God, restraining them from idleness and profanation of the Sabbath, 3dly, that you freely and readily entertain any honest men, into your church, estate and society, though with great infirmities and difference of judgment; taking heed of too great straitness and singularity even in that particular. 4thly, that there be fervent love and close cleaving together among you that are fearers of God, without secret whispering or undermining one of another, and without contempt or neglect of such as are weak and helpless, if honest, amongst you. This do, and in all things be humble, cheerful and thankful; that if you cannot grow rich in this world, yet you may be rich in grace; and if you can send us no other treasure, yet let all that visit you, bring from you the fame of honesty, religion and godliness, which we trust, shall comfort us more than all else you can send us in this world.

At a word, though we be detected of folly, ignorance, want of judgment, yet let no man charge us with dishonesty, looseness or unconscionableness; but though we lose our labours or adventures, or charges, yea our lives; yet let us not lose one jot of our innocence, integrity, holiness, fear and comfort with God.

And, thus ceasing for this time to trouble you further; praying God to bless and prosper you, and sanctify all your crosses and losses, that they may turn to your great profit and comfort in the end, with hearty salutations to you all, we lovingly take leave of you, from London, April 7, 1624.

Your assured lovers and friends,

James Sherley, Thomas Fletcher,
Thomas Brewer, John Ling,
William Collier, William, Thomas,
Joseph Pocok, Robert Reayne.

[Now follows the first letters we received after the breach; for Mr. Thornell and the rest never replied nor writ more unto us, being partly ashamed of what they done and written.]

To our beloved friends Mr. William, Bradford, Mr. Isaac Allerton, Mr. William Brewster, and the rest of the general society of Plymouth in New England, salutations.

Though the thing we feared be come upon us and the evils we strove against, have overtaken us; yet cannot we forget you, nor our friendship and fellowship, which, together we have had some years; wherein though our expressions have been small, yet our hearty affections towards you (unknown by face) have been no less than to our nearest friends, yea even to our own selves. And though your and our friend, Mr. Winslow, can tell you the estate of things here, and what hath befallen us; yet lest we should seem to neglect you, to whom by a wonderful providence of God, we are so nearly united; we have thought good once more to write unto you, and the arguments of our letter must consist of these three points, first to shew you what is here befallen, 2dly, the reason and cause of that which is fallen, 3rdly, our purposes and desires towards you hereafter.

The former course for the generality here is wholly dissolved from that course which was held. And whereas you and we, were formerly sharers, and partners in all voyages and dealings, this way is now so no more, but you and we are left to bethink ourselves, what course to take in the future, that your lives and our monies be not lost. And this, as ourselves first saw, so have we begun to practice, as we thought best for your and our safety for hereafter; and it standeth you no less in hand seriously to consider what is best to do, that you may both continue good conscience with God and procure your best safety in this world.

The reasons and causes of this alteration, have been these first and mainly, the many crosses, and losses and abuses by sea and seamen, which have caused us to run into so much charge, and debts and engagements, as our estates and means were not able to go on without impoverishing ourselves, and much hindering if not spoiling our trades and callings here; except our estates had been greater or our associates had cloven better to us. 2dly, As here hath been a faction and siding amongst us now more than two years; so now there is an utter breach and sequestration amongst us, and in two parts of us, a full dissertion, and forsaking of you, without any intent or purpose of meddling more with you.

And though we are persuaded the main cause of their this doing is want of money (for need whereof men use to make many excuses) yet other things are by many pretended, and not without some colour urged, which are these: 1st, A distaste of you there, for that you are (as they affirm) Brownists, condemning all other churches, and persons but yourselves and those in your way, and you are contentious, cruel and hard hearted, among your neighbours and towards such as in all points both civil and religious, jump not with you. And that you are negligent, careless, wasteful, unthrifty, and suffer all general goods, and affairs to go at six and sevens and spend your time in idleness and talking and conferring, and care not what be wasted worn and torn out, whilst all things come so easily, and so cheap unto you. 2dly, A distaste and personal contempt of us for taking your parts and striving to defend you, and make the best of all matters touching you, insomuch as it is hard to say whether you or we are least loved of them.

Now what use either you or we may make of these things, it remaineth to be considered; and the more, for that we know the hand of God to be present in all these things, and he no doubt would admonish us of something which is not yet so looked to and taken to heart as it should. And although it be now too late for us, or you, to prevent and stay these things, yet is it not too late to exercise patience, wisdom and conscience, in bearing them, and in carrying ourselves in and under them for time to come. And as we ourselves stand ready to embrace all occasions that may tend to the furtherance of so hopeful a work; rather admiring at what is, than grudging for what is not, so it must rest still in you to make all good again. And if in nothing else you can be approved, yet let your honesty and conscience be still approved, and lose not one jot of your innocence amidst your many crosses and afflictions.

And surely if you upon this alteration behave yourselves wisely and go on fairly, as men whose hopes is not in this life; you shall need no other weapon to wound your adversaries; for when your righteousness is revealed as the light, they shall cover their faces with shame, that causelessly have sought your overthrow.

And although (we hope) you need not our council in these things, having learned of God how to behave yourselves, in all estates in this world, yet a word for your advice and direction, to spur those forward, which we hope run already.

And first, seeing our generality here is dissolved, let yours be the more firm; and do not you like carnal people (which run into inconveniences and evils by examples) but rather be warned by your harms, to cleave faster together hereafter; take heed of long and sharp disputes and oppositions, give no passage to the waters, no not a tittle; let not hatred or heartburning be harboured in the breast of any of you one moment, but forgive and forget all former failings and abuses, and renew your love and friendship together daily. There is often more sound friendship and sweeter fellowship in afflictions and crosses than in prosperity and favours; and there is reason for it, because envy flieth away when there is nothing but necessities to be looked on; but it is always a bold *guest* where prosperity shews itself.

And although we here which are hedged about with so many favours and helps in worldly things and comforts; forget friendship and love and fall out often times for trifles; yet you must not do so, but must in these things turn a new leaf and be of another spirit. We here can fall out with a friend and lose him today, and find another tomorrow; but you cannot do so, you have no such choice, you must make much of them you have, and count him a very good friend, which is not a professed enemy. We have a trade and custom of tale bearing, whispering and changing of old friends for new, and these things with us are incurable. But you which do as it were begin a new world and lay the foundation of sound piety and humanity for others to follow, must suffer no such weeds in your garden, but nip them in the head, and cast them out forever; and must follow peace and study quietness, having fervent love amongst yourselves as a perfect and entire bond to uphold you when all else fails you. And although we have written much to you heretofore to provoke to union and love as the only way to make you stand, and without which all would come to nothing; so now you are much more to be provoked thereunto, since you are left, rather to be spectators to the eye than objects to the hand, and stand most need one of another, at home when foreign help is so much decayed and weakened.

And if any amongst you, for all that, have still a withdrawing heart, and will be all to himself, and nothing to his neighbour, let him think of these things, 1st. The providence of God in bringing you there together. 2d, His marvellous preserving you from so many dangers, the particulars whereof you know and must never forget. 3d, The hopes that yet are of effecting somewhat for yourselves and more for your posterity if hand join in hand. 4th, The woful estate of him which is alone, especially in a wilderness. 5th, The succour and comfort which the generality can daily afford, having built houses, planted corn, framed boats, erected salt works, obtained cattle, swine, and pulling, [1] together with the diverse varieties of trades and faculties employed by sea and land, the gains of every one stretching itself unto all whilst they are in the general: but such as withdraw themselves tempting God and despising their neighbours, must look for no share or part in any of these things; but as they will be a commonwealth alone, so alone they must work, and alone they must eat, and alone they must be sick and die, or else languishing under the frustration of their vain hopes, alone return to England, and there to help all cry out of the country and the people; counting the one fruitless and the other merciless; when indeed their own folly, pride, and idleness is the cause of all which never weigh either the providence of God, the conscience of their duty, nor care for their neighbours, or themselves, further than to grate upon their friends; as if other men owed them all things, and they owed no man any thing. 6th, The conscience of making restitution, and paying those debts and charges which hath befallen to bring you there, and send those things to you, which you have had, must hold you together; and for him that withdraws himself from the general; we look upon him, as upon a man, who, having served his turn, and fulfiled his desire, cares not what becomes of others, neither maketh conscience of any debt, or duty at all, but thinketh to slide away under secret colours, to abuse and deceive his friends; and against whom we need say little, seeing the Lord will never cease to curse his course.

And albeit, the company here as a company hath lost you; you know when Saul left David, yea, and pursued him, yet David did not abuse his allegiance and loyalty to him, no more should you; the evil of us here, cannot justify any evil in you, but you must still do your duty, though we neglect ours. 2dly, Indeed we are persuaded, it is in the most of the adventurers rather want of power, than will, that maketh them break off; they having gone as far as they can in the business, and are as sorry that they cannot go forward as you are offended that they do not go forward, yea, and the pretences of those which have the most colours, we are persuaded, proceed more from weakness of the purse, than fear of any thing else; and the want of money is such a grievous sickness now-a-days, as that it makes men rave and cry out, they cannot tell for what. 3dly, And in a word we think it but reason, that all such things as these, are appertaining to the general, be kept and preserved together, and rather increased daily, than any way dispersed or embezzled away, for any private ends or intents whatsoever. 4thly, That after your necessities are served, you gather together such commodities as the country yields, and send them over to pay debts and clear engagements here, which are not less than £1400. All which debts, besides adventures, have been made about general commodities and implements, and for which divers of us, stand more or less engaged. And we dare say of you, that you will do the best you can to free us, and unburden us, that for your sakes, and help, are so much hazarded in our estates, and names. 5thly, If there be any that will withdraw himself from the general, as he must not have, nor use any of the general's goods, so it is but reason that he give sufficient security for payment of so much of the debts as his part Cometh to; which how much it will come to, upon a person, or family is quickly counted; and since we require but men's faithful endeavours, and cannot obtain them, let none think much if we require other security than fair words and promises, of such men as make no more conscience of their words and ways.

If any amongst you shall object against us, either our long delays in our supplies heretofore, or our too much jollity in spending sometimes at our meetings more than perhaps needed; that will prove but trifling, for we could also find fault with the idleness and sloth of many amongst you, which have made all the rest go forward slowly, as also we could find fault with your liberality, and largeness also, when it might have been otherwise; but all such matters must still be left to the discretion and conscience of either side, knowing that where many have a hand in such business, there will not want some, that are too timerous and slack; as also that in matters of note, something must be done for form and credit. And for ourselves we think there hath hardly in our days; been a business, of this note, and fame, carried by Londoners, with twice the expense in by matters that this hath been; and therefore let each man rather seek to mend himself, than hastily to cast in objections against others.

In a word, since it thus still falleth out, that all things between us, are as you see, let us all endeavour to keep a fair and honest course, and see what time will bring forth, and how God in his providence will work for us. We still are persuaded, you are the people, that must make a plantation, and erect a city in those remote places, when all others fail, and return; and your experience of God's providence and preservation of you is such, that we hope your hearts will not now fail you, though your friends should forsake you (which we ourselves shall not do whilst we live, so long as your honesty so well appeareth) yet surely help would arise from some other place, whilst you wait on God with uprightness, though we should leave you also.

To conclude, as you are especially now to renew your love one to another; so we advise you, as your friends to these particulars. First let all sharpness, reprehensions, and corrections, of opposite persons, be still used sparingly, and take no advantage against any, for any by respects; but rather wait for their mending amongst you, than to mend them yourselves by thrusting them away, of whom there is any hope of good to be had. 2d, Make your corporation, as formal as you can, under the name of the Society of Plymouth in New England, allowing some peculiar privileges, to all the members thereof, according to the tenure of the patents. 3d, Let your practises and course in religion in the church, be made complete, and full; let all that fear God amongst you, join themselves thereunto without delay; and let all the ordinances of God be used completely in the church without longer waiting. upon uncertainties, or keeping the gap open for opposites. 4ly, Let the worship and service of God be strictly kept on the Sabbath, and both together, and asunder let the day be sanctified; and let your care be seen on the working days every where and upon all occasions to set forward the service of God. And lastly, be you all entreated to walk so circumspectly and carry yourselves so uprightly in all your ways, as that no man may make just exceptions against you; and more especially that the favour and countenance of God may be so towards you, as that you may find abundant joy and peace even amidst tribulations, that you may say with David, *though my father and my mother should forsake me; yet the Lord will take me up.*

We have sent you some cattle, cloth, hose, shoes, leather, &c. but in another nature than formerly, as it stood us in hand to do; we have committed them to the custody and charge of, as our factors, Mr. Allerton and Mr. Winslow, at whose discretion they are to be sold and commodities, taken for them as is fitting. And it standeth you in need the more carefully to look to, and make much of all your commodities, by how much the more they are chargeable to you, and though we hope you shall not want things necessary, so we think the harder they are got, the more carefully they will be husbanded. Good friends, as you buy them, keep a decorum in distributing them, and let none have varieties, and things for delight, when others want for their mere necessities, and have an eye rather on your ill deservings at God's hand, than upon the failings of your friends towards you; and wait on him with patience, and good conscience; rather admiring his mercies, (than repining at his crosses,) with the assurance of faith, that what is wanting here shall be made up in glory a thousand fold. Go on good friends, comfortably pluck up your hearts cheerfully, and quit yourselves like men, in all your difficulties, that notwithstanding all displeasure and threats of men, yet the work may go on which you are about, and not be neglected, which is so much for the glory of God, and the furtherance of our Countrymen, as that a man may with more comfort spend his life in it; than live the life of Methuselah in wasting the plenty of a tilled land, or eating the fruit of a grown tree.

Thus having not time to write further unto you, leaving other things to the relation of our friends; with all hearty salutations to you all, and hearty prayers, for you all, we lovingly take our leave this 18th of December, 1624.

Your assured friends to our power,

James Sherley, (sick)
William Collier,
Thomas Fletcher,
Robert Holland.

[This letter was wrote with Mr. Cushman's hand; and it is likely was penned by him at the other's request.]

Mr. Cushman to *Gov.* Bradford.

Sir, *December* 22,

1624.

My hearty love remembered unto you, and unto your wife, with trust of your healths, and contentment amidst so many difficulties. I am now to write unto you, from my friend, and from myself, my friend and your friend. Mr. Sherley, who lieth even at the point of death, intreated me, even with tears, to write to excuse him, and signify how it was with him; he remembers his hearty, and as he thinks his last, salutations to you, and all the rest, who love our common cause. And if God does again raise him up, he will be more for you (I am persuaded) than ever he was. His unfeigned love towards us, hath been such, as I cannot indeed express; and though he be a man not swayed with passion, or led by uninformed affections, yet hath he cloven to us still amidst all persuasions of opposites; and could not be moved to have an evil thought of us, for all their clamours. His patience and contentment in being oppressed hath been much; he hath sometimes lent £800 at one time, for other men to adventure in this business, all to draw them on; and hath indeed by his free heartedness been the only glue of the company And if God should take him now away, I scarce think much more would be done, save as to enquire at the dividend what is to be had.

He saith he hath received the tokens you sent, and thanks you for them: he hath sent you a cheese, &c. Also he hath sent an heifer to the plantation, to begin a stock for the poor. There is also a bull and three or four jades, to be sold unto you, with many other things, for apparel and other uses; which are committed to Mr. Alerton and Mr. Winslow, who as factors are to sell them to you; and it was fitter for many reasons, to make them factors than yourself, as I hope you will easily conceive.

And I hope though the first project cease, yet it shall be never the worse for you, neither will any man be discouraged, but wait on God, using the good means you can. I have no time to write many things unto you; I doubt not but upon the hearing of this alteration some discontent may arise, but the Lord I hope will teach you the way which you shall choose. For myself as I have laboured by all means, to hold things here together, so I have patiently suffered this alteration; and do yet hope it shall be good for you all, if you be not too rash, and hasty; which if any be, let them take heed they reap not the fruit of their own vanities.

But for you, good Sir, I hope you will do nothing rashly, neither will you be swayed, by misreports, beside your ordinary course, but will persuade who may be, to patience, and peace; and to the bearing of labours, and crosses in love together.

I hope the failings of your friends here, will make you the more friendly one to another, that so all our hopes may not be dashed. Labour to settle things, both in your civil, and religious courses, as firm, and as full as you can. Lastly, I must intreat you still, to have a care of my son, as of your own; and I shall rest bound unto you, I pray you let him sometime practice writing. I hope the next ships to come to you; in the mean space and ever, the Lord be all your direction, and turn all our crosses and troubles to his own glory, and our comforts, and give you to walk so wisely, and holily, as none may justly say, but they have always found you honestly minded, though never so poor. Salute all our friends, and supply, I pray you, what, if failing in my letters. From London, *December* 22, *A.D.* 1624.

Thus were his last letters. And now we lost the help of a wise and faithful friend, he wrote of the sickness, and probability of the death of another; but knew not that his own was so near, what cause have we therefore ever to be ready! He purposed to be with us the next ships, but the Lord did otherwise dispose; and had appointed him a greater journey, to a better place. He was now taken from these troubles into which (by this division) we were so deeply plunged. And heer I must leave him to rest with the Lord. And will proceed to other letters which will further shew our proceedings and how things went on.

Gov. Bradford to *Mr.* Cushman

Loving and kind friend, I most heartily thank you; and would be right glad to see you here, with many other of our old and dear friends, that we might strengthen, and comfort one another, after our many troubles, travels, and hardships. I long greatly for friends of Leyden, but I fear, I shall now scarce ever see them, save in heaven; but the will of the Lord be done. We have rid ourselves of the company of many of those, who have been so troublesome unto us; though I fear we are not yet rid of the troubles themselves. I hear Culdom [2] comes himself into England; the which if he do, beware of him, for he is very malicious, and much threatens you; thinking he hath some advantage by some words you have spoken. Touching his factious doings here, and our proceedings with him, I refer you for it, and many other things to the relations of Captain Standish, whom we have thought most meet for sundry reasons, to send at this time. I pray you be as helpful to him as you can; especially in making our provisions, for therein he hath the least skill.

We have sent by this first ship, a good parcel of commodities, to wit: As much beaver and other furs, as will amount to upwards of £277, sterling, at the rates they were sold the last year. In part of payment of those goods, they and you sent to be sold to us. But except we may have things, both more serviceable, and at better rates, we shall never be able to rub through; therefore if we could have some ready money disbursed to buy things at the best hand, it would be greatly in our way. Special care is to be had of procuring us good trucking stuff, for without it we can do nothing; the reason why heretofore we have got so little is, because we never had any that was good till Mr. Winslow brought some over.

Our people will never agree, any way again to unite with the Company; who have cast them off with such reproach and contempt; and also returned their bills, and all debts upon their heads. But as for those our loving friends, who have, and still do stick to us, and are deeply engaged for us, and are most careful of our goods, for our parts we will ever be ready to do any thing, that shall be thought equal and mete.

But I think it will be best, to press, a clearance with the Company; either by coming to a dividend, or some other indifferent course or composition; for the longer we hang and continue in this confused and lingering condition, the worse it will be, for it takes away all heart and courage, from men, to do any thing. For notwithstanding any persuasion to the contrary, many protest they will never build houses, fence grounds, or plant fruits for those, who not only forsake them, but use them as enemies, lading them with reproach and contumely. Nay they will rather ruin that, which is done, than they should possess it. Whereas if they knew what they should trust to, the place would quickly grow and flourish with plenty, for they never felt the sweetness of the country till this year; and not only we but all planters in the land begin to do it. Let us be as little engaged about fishing, or any other projects, as you can, to draw us away from our own employments for they will be the most beneficial unto us. I suppose to spend our own salt and to employ as many of our own boats as we can, will be best for us. If we had but kept two a trading this year, it would have been twice as good as our fishing; though I hope the ships will return with good voyages.

Your son and all of us, are in good health, (blessed be God) he received the things you sent him. I hope God will make him a good man. My wife remembers her love unto you, and thanks you for her spice. Billington still rails against you, and threatens to arrest you, I know not wherefore; he is a knave, and so will live and die. Mr. John Pearce wrote he would make a 17parliamentary matter, about our grand patent, I pray you wish our friends to look to it, for I mistrust him, I perceive there passeth intelligence between Mr. Weston, and him, by means of Mr. Hix. He is come again hither, and is not yet quiet about that £100. The Lord hath so graciously disposed, that when our opposites thought, that many would have followed their faction, they so distasted their palpable dishonest dealings, that they stuck more firmly unto us, and joined themselves to the Church. But time cuts me off, for other things; I refer you to my other more general, and larger letters, and so with my renewed salutations, and best love remembered unto you. I commend you and all our affairs, to the guidance of the Most High, and so rest, your assured loving friend,

WILLIAM BRADFORD.

New-Plymouth, June 9, 1625.

[*Mr. Cushman died before this letter arrived.*]

Next follows a letter to the Council of New England, wherein their help was supplicated.

To the right Honourable his Majesty's Council for New England these be, &c.

Right Honourable,   *June 28, A.D.*
1625.

The assurance we have of your noble dispositions to releave the oppressions of the innocent, doth cause us to fly unto you, as to a sanctuary, in this our just cause. It hath pleased the divine Providence to bring us into this place where we inhabit under your government, wherein we now have resided almost these five years, having put some life, into this then dreaded, design, made way for others and to all that are here, have been and still are their bulwark and defence.

Many necessities we have undergone, incident to the raw, and immature beginnings of such great exertions, and yet are subject to many more. We are many people, consisting of all sorts, as well women children, as men; and are now left, and forsaken of our adventurers, who will neither supply us with necessaries for our subsistence, nor suffer others that would be willing; neither can we be at liberty to deal with others, or provide for ourselves, but they keep us tied to them, and yet they will be loose from us; they have not only cast us off, but entered into particular course of trading, and have by violence, and force, taken at their pleasure, our possession at Cape Ann. Traducing us with unjust, and dishonest clammours abroad, disturbing our peace at home; and some of them threatening, that if ever we grow to any good estate they will then nip us in the head. Which discouragements do cause us to slack our diligence, and care to build and plant, and cheerfully perform our other employments, not knowing for whom we work whether friends or enemies.

Our humble suit therefore to your good lordships and honours is, that seeing they have so unjustly forsaken us, that you would vouchsafe to convene them before you, and take such order, as we may be free from them; and they come to a division with us, that we and ours may be delivered from their evil intents against us. So shall we comfortably go forward, with the work we have in hand, as first to God's glory, and the honour of our king; so to the good satisfaction of your honours, and for our present, common, and after good of our posterity. The prosecution of this, we have committed to our agent Captain Myles Standish, who attends your Honourable pleasures.

The great God of heaven and earth, who hath put into your hearts, to travail in this honourable action, strengthen your hearts and hands hereunto; and gave his blessing answerable to your worthy endeavours. In all humbleness we commit ourselves to your honourable direction and protection. And rest with the knowledge, consent and humble request of the whole plantation ever at commandment.

WILLIAM BRADFORD, Gov.

But by reason of the great plague which raged this year in London, of which so many thousands died weekly, Captain Standish could do nothing either with the Council of New England, or any other hereabout, for there was no Courts kept or scarce any commerce held, the city being in a sort desolate, by the fervent pestilence, and flight of so many. So as he was forced to return; having by the help of some friends (with much ado, and great both trouble and peril to himself) procured a convenient supply; which he brought with him to save our greatest necessities.

A Letter of Mr. Fletcher's showing his great loss of the little James; she and the beaver in her, which was sent for the goods we bought the other year, being for the most part his; and was taken by the Turks to his utter undoing.

To his loving friends Mr. Bradford, *Mr.* Allerton, and *Mr.* Winslow, *salutations, &c.*

London, November 25, 1625.

My last unto you, was of the death of Mr. Robinson and what else then needful, since which I have received divers letters from you, and perceive at large what things you want, and do desire, and with what grievances you have been oppressed. And had the Lord so disposed, as to have sent us the pinace home, no doubt myself would have seen you well supplied; and some of your grievances should have been removed, but so it is, that all power therein to do you good, is wholly (by God's providence) taken from me. And so I much fear, that this year you will hardly be able to do yourselves, or your friends much good, but patience, &c.

And for other affairs either touching myself, and my necessities I am put unto, besides disgrace and reproach from many; as also touching the rest of our adventurers, who fall from me like the water brooks, as Job complains. I say for all these things, and many more here passed, I refer you to your Agent, and my loving friend. Captain Standish, who can certify you all things at large; as also of the feigned and perfidious dealings of Mr. John Peirce towards me, and others, who now hath manifest himself, at least to some, not to mind that good for you, or us, as was fit, and oft pretended. But all these things, they come from God for diverse reasons as first, to humble us, and subdue our corruption; 2d, to win us from the world. 3d, to add unto our joy to come. 4th, to shew forth the great power, goodness and mercy of our God, in preserving us in, and delivering us out of the same. Wherefore let us be patient, and thankful without murmuring. Amen, Amen. And so with my hearty well wishes for you all, and your general good; for which I shall often approach to the throne of grace, and expect the like from you, and so I leave you with this salutation, fare you well, my brethren all, fare you well; and God of grace and peace, bless you, and your posterities to the coming of Jesus Christ. Amen.

Your loving friend, in what I can.

THOMAS FLETCHER.

I will next insert some letters from our friends at Leyden, written this year; and first, a letter of Mr. White's to myself, in which the heavy tidings of our beloved and able pastor's death and the manner of it, is declared.

To his loving friend, Mr. William Bradford, *Governour of Plymouth, in New England, these be, &c.*

Loving and kind friends, &c. I know not whether ever this will come to your hands, or miscarry, as other of my letters have done; yet in regard of the Lord's dealing with us here, I have had a great desire to write unto you; knowing your desire to bear a part with us, both in our joys and sorrows, as we do with you.

These therefore are to give you to understand, that it hath pleased the Lord to take out of this veil of tears, your, and our loving and faithful pastor, and my dear brother, Mr. John Robinson, who was sick some, eight days, beginning first to be sick on a Saturday morning, yet the next day, being the Lord's day he taught us twice, and the week after grew every day weaker, than other, yet felt no pain but weakness, all the time of his sickness; the physick he took wrought kindly, in man's judgment, yet he grew every day weaker than other, feeling little or no pain, yet sensible, till the very last. Who fell sick the twenty second of February, and departed this life the first of March. He had a continual inward ague, which brought the - but I thank the Lord, was free of the plague, so that all his friends could come freely to him. And if either prayers, tears, or means would have saved his life, he had not gone hence. But he having faithfully finished his course, and performed his work, which the Lord had appointed him here to perform; he now rests with the Lord, in eternal happiness. We wanting him and all church Governours, not having one at present that is a governing officer amongst us. Now for ourselves here left (I mean the whole Church) we still, by the mercy of God, continue and hold close together in peace and quietness, and so I hope we shall do though we be very weak;. wishing (if such were the will of God) that you and we were again together in one, either there or here, but seeing it is the will of the Lord, thus to dispose of things, we must labour with patience to rest contented till it please the Lord otherwise to dispose of things.

For news at present here, is not much worth the writing, only as in England we have lost our old King who departed this life about a month ago, so here we have lost Grave Morrice, the old Prince here, who both departed this life, since my brother Robinson; and as in England we have a new King, Charles, of whom there is great hope of good; the King is making ready about one hundred sail of ships, the end is not yet certain, but they will be ready to go to sea very shortly; the King himself goes to see them once in fourteen „days. So here likewise we have made Prince Hendrick General, in his brother's place, who is now with the Grave of Mansfield with a great army, close by the enemy, to free Breda, if it be possible, which the enemy hath besieged now some nine or ten months; but how it will fall out at last, is yet uncertain, the Lord give good success if it be his will. And thus fearing lest this will not come to your hands, hoping as soon as I hear of a convenient messenger, to write more at large, and to send you a letter which my brother Robinson sent to London; to have gone to some of you, but coming too late, was brought back again. And so for this time I cease further to trouble you, and rest.

Your assured loving friend,

ROGER WHITE.

Leyden, April 28, Anno 1625.

A letter of Thomas Blossom's to myself and Mr. Brewster, touching the same things as followeth.

Beloved Sir,

Kind salutations, &c. I have thought good to write to you, concerning the cause as it standeth both with you and us; we see, alas I what frustrations and disappointments it pleaseth the Lord to send in this our course, good in itself and according to godliness taken in hand and for good and lawful ends, who yet pleaseth not to prosper us we see, for reasons best known to himself: And which also nearly concerns us to consider of, whether we have sought the Lord in it, as we ought, or not; that the Lord hath singularly preserved life in the business to great admiration, giveth me good hope that he will (if our sins hinder not) in his appointed time, give a happy end unto it. On the contrary when I consider how it pleaseth the Lord to cross those means that should bring us together, being now as far off or farther than ever, in our apprehension; as also to take that means away, which would have -been so comfortable unto us in that course, both for wisdom of council as also for our singular help in our course of godliness, whom the Lord (as it were) took away even as fruit falleth before it was ripe, (he means Mr. Robinson) when neither length of days, nor infirmity of body, did seem to call for his end. The Lord even then took him away, as it were in his anger, whom if tears would have held, he had remained to this day. The loss of his ministry was very great unto me, for I ever counted myself happy in the enjoyment of it, notwithstanding all the crosses and losses otherwise I sustained. Yet indeed the manner of his taking away hath more troubled me, as fearing the Lord's anger in it, that, as I said, in the ordinary course of things might still have remained, as also, the singular service he might have yet done in the church of God. Alas, dear friends, our state and cause in religion! by his death being wholly destitute of any that may defend our cause as it should against our adversaries. That we may take up that doleful complaint in the Psalm, that there is no prophet left among us, nor any that knoweth how long.

Alas! you would fain have had him with you, and he would as fain have come to you; many letters and much speech hath been about his coming to you, but never any solid course propounded for his going; if the course propounded the last year had appeared to have been certain, he would have gone though with two or three families., I know no man amongst us knew his mind better than I did, about those things; he was loath to leave the church, yet I know also, that he would have accepted the worst conditions which in the largest extent of a good conscience could be taken, to have come to you. For myself and all such others as have formerly minded coming, it is much what the same, if the Lord afford means. We only know how things are with you by your letters, but how things stand in England we have received no letters of any thing, and it was November before we received yours. If we come at all unto you, the means to enable us so to do must come from you. For the state of our church, and how it is with us and of our people, it is wrote of by Mr. White. Thus praying you to pardon my boldness with you in writing as I do, I commend you to the keeping of the Lord, desiring, if he see it good, and that I might be serviceable unto the business, that I were with you. God hath taken away my son, that was with me in the ship, when I went back again; I have only two children which were born since I left you: Fare you well.

Yours to his power,

THOMAS BLOSSOM.

Leyden, December 15, *Anno* 1625.

To his very loving friend, Mr. William Bradford, Governour of Plymouth in New England, these be.

My loving and kind friend, and brother in the Lord; my own and my wife's true love and hearty salutations to yourself and yours and all the rest of our loving friends with you; hoping in the Lord of your good healths, which I beseech him long to continue for the glory of his name and good of his people. Concerning your kind letter to the church, it was read publicly; whereunto (by the church) I send you here inclosed an answer. Concerning my brother Robinson's sickness and death and our practice, I wrote you at large, some five or six months since; but lest it should miscarry, I have now written to Mr. Brewster thereof, to whom I refer you. Now concerning your course of choosing your Governours yearly, and in special of their choosing yourself year after year, as I conceive they still do, and Mr. Allerton your assistant; howsoever I think it the best way that can be, so long as it please the Lord to continue your lives, and so good Governours offer you; yet, considering man's mortality, whose breath is in his nostrils, and the evils of the times wherein we live, in which it is ordinarily seen that worse follow them that are good, I think it would be a safer course, for after time, the government was sometime removed from one to another; so the assistant one year might be Governour next and a new assistant chosen in his place either of such as have or

22

have not been in office; sometimes one, sometimes another, as it shall seem most fit to the corporation. My reasons are, first, because other officers that come after you, will look (especially if they be ambitiously minded) for the same privileges and continuance you have had; and if he have it not, will take great offence, as though unworthy of the place, and so greatly disgraced, whom to continue, might be very dangerous, and hazard (at least) the overthrow of all; men not looking so much at the reasons why others were so long continued as at the custom. 2dly, because others that are unexperienced in government might learn by experience; and so there might be fit and able men continually, when it pleaseth the Lord to take any away. 3dly, by this means, you may establish the things begun, or done before; for the Governour this year, that was assistant last, will in likelihood, rather ratify and confirm, and go on with that he had a hand in the beginning of, when he was assistant, than otherwise, or persuade the new to it; whereas new Governours, especially when there are factions, will many times overthrow that which is done by the former, and so scarcely any thing goeth forward for the general good; neither that I see, can this be any prejudice to the corporation; for the new may always have the counsel and advice of the old, for their direction, though they be out of office; these things I make bold to put to your godly wisdom and discretion, intreating you to pardon my boldness therein; and so leave it to your discretion to make use of as you see it fitting, not having written the least inkling hereof to any other. Now I entreat you, at your best leisure to write to me, how you think it will in likelihood go with your civil and church estate; whether there be hope of the continuance of both, or either; or whether you fear any alteration to be attempted in either; the reason of this my request is, the fear of some amongst us (the which if that hinder not, I think will come unto you) occasioned partly by your letter to your father in law, Mr. May, wherein you write of the troubles you have had with some, who it is like (having the times and friends on their sides) will work you what mischiefs they can; and that they may do much, many here do fear: And partly by reason of this king's proclamation, dated the 13th of May last, in which he saith, that his full resolution is, to the end that there may be one uniform course of government, in, and through all his whole monarchy; that the government of Virginia shall immediately depend on himself, and not be committed to any company or corporation, etc. so that some conceive he will have both the same civil and ecclesiastical government that is in England, which occasioneth their fear. I desire you to write your thoughts of these things, for the satisfying of others; for my own part and some others, we durst rely upon you for that, who we persuade ourselves, would not be thus earnest, for our pastor and church to come to you; if you feared the danger of being suppressed. Thus desiring you to pardon my boldness, and remember us in your prayers; I for this time and ever, commit you and all your affairs to the Almighty, and rest

Your assured loving friend

And brother in the Lord,
ROGER WHITE.

Leyden, Dec. 1. *Anno* 1625.

P. S. The church would entreat you to continue your writing to them, which is very comfortable.

To our most dear, and entirely beloved brethren, Mr. William Bradford and Mr. William Brewster, grace mercy and true peace be multiplied, from God our Father, through our Lord Jesus Christ. Amen.

Most dear Christian friends and brethren, as it is no small grief unto you, so is it no less unto us, that we are constrained to live thus disunited each from other, especially considering our affections each unto other, for the mutual edifying and comfort of both, in these evil days wherein we live: if it pleased the Lord to bring us again together, than which as no outward thing could be more comfortable unto us, or is more desired of us, if the Lord see it good; so see we no hope of means of accomplishing the same, except it come from you, and therefore, must with patience rest in the work and will of God, performing our duties to him and you assunder; whom we are not any way able to help, but by our continual prayers to him for you, and sympathy of affections with you, for the troubles which befal you; till it please the Lord to reunite us again. But our dearly beloved brethren, concerning your kind and respective letter, howsoever written by one of you, yet as we continue with the consent (at least in affection) of you both, although we cannot answer your desire and expectation, by reason it hath pleased the Lord to take to himself out of this miserable world our dearly beloved pastor, yet for ourselves we are minded as formerly, to come unto you, when and as the Lord affordeth means, though we see little hope thereof at present, as being unable of ourselves, and that our friends will help us we see little hope. And now, brethren, what shall we say further unto you; our desires and prayers to God, is (if such were his good will and pleasure) we might be reunited for the edifying and mutual comfort of both, which, when he sees fit, he will accomplish. In the mean time, we commit you unto him and to the word of his grace; whom we beseech to guide and direct both you and us, in all his ways, according to that, his word, and to bless all our lawful endeavours, for the glory of his name and good of his people. Salute, we pray you, all the church and brethren with you to whom we would have sent this letter. If we knew it could not be prejudicial unto you, as we hope it cannot;

24

yet fearing the worst, we thought fit either to direct it to you, our two beloved brethen, leaving it to your goodly wisdom and discretion, to manifest our mind to the rest of our loving friends and brethren, as you see most convenient. And thus intreating you to remember us in your prayers, as we also do you; we for this time commend you and all your affairs to the direction and protection of the Almighty, and rest.

Your assured loving friends

And brethren in the Lord,
FRANCIS JESSOPP,
THOMAS NASH,
THOMAS BLOSSOM,
ROGER WHITE,
RICHARD MAISTERSON.

Leyden, Nov. 30, *A.D.* 1625.

Before I pass to other things, I will here insert a letter of Mr. Robinson's, which, though it is out of place, yet coming now to hand, I thought better to put it here, than to omit it. It was written to the church as followeth:

To the church of God, at Plymouth, in New England.

Much beloved brethren, neither the distance of place, nor distinction of body, can at all either dissolve or weaken that bond of true Christian affection in which the Lord by his spirit hath tied us together. My continual prayers are to the Lord for you; my most earnest desire is unto you; from whom I will not longer keep (if God will) than means can be procured to bring with me the wives and children of divers of you and the rest of your brethren, whom I could not leave behind me without great, both injury to you and them, and offence to God and all men. The death of so many our dear friends and brethren; oh I how grievous hath it been to you to bear, and to us to take knowledge of, which, if it could be mended with lamenting, could not sufficiently be bewailed; but we must go unto them and they shall not return unto us: And how many even of us, God hath taken away here, and in England, since your departure, you may elsewhere take knowledge. But the same God has tempered judgment with mercy, as otherwise, so in sparing the rest, especially those by whose godly and wise government, you may be, and (I know) are so much helped. In a battle it is not looked for but that divers should die; it is thought well for a side, if it get the victory, though with the loss of divers, if not too many or too great. God, I hope, hath given you the victory, after many difficulties, for yourselves and others; though I doubt not, but many do and will remain for you and us all to strive with. Brethren, I hope I need not exhort you to obedience unto those whom God hath set over you, in church and commonwealth, and to the Lord in them. It is a christian's honour, to give honour according to men's places; and his liberty, to serve God in faith, and his brethren in love orderly and with a willing and free heart. God forbid, I should need to exhort you to peace, which is the bond of perfection, and by which all good is tied together, and without which it is scattered. Have peace with God first, by faith in his promises, good conscience kept in all things, and oft renewed by repentance; and so, one with another, for his sake, who is, though three, one; and for Christ's sake who is one, and as you are called by one spirit to one hope. And the God of peace and grace and all goodness be with you, in all the fruits thereof, plenteously upon your heads, now and for ever. All your brethren here, remember you with great love, a general token whereof they have sent you.

Yours ever in the Lord,

Leyden, (Holland) June 30, *Anno* 1621.   JOHN ROBIN-SON.

This next year being Anno. 1626, we sent Mr. Allerton into England, partly to make some supply for us, and to see if he could make any reasonable composition with the adventurers and because we well knew that nothing can be done without money, we gave him an order to procure some, binding ourselves to make payment thereof, as followeth:

Know all men by these presents, that whereas we William Bradford, Governour of Plymouth in New England, and William Brewster, Capt. Miles Standish, Isaac Allerton, Samuel Fuller, Edward Winslow, John Jeney, John Howland, and John Allden; being all inhabitants of Plymouth, aforesaid, are for ourselves, and divers others, our associates, &c. And whereas the said Isaac Allerton (by God's providence) for the necessary occasions of the colony abovesaid, is bound for England; and whereas divers of us above named, have acquainted divers of our worthy and approved friends (by our letters) [3] with our raw and weak estate, and want of ability of ourselves to manage so great an action, as the upholding of the plantation aforesaid If therefore God shall move the heart or hearts of any of our friends, in compassion of our wants and present straits, to lend us above named, the sum of one hundred pounds sterling, for the space of two years, upon any such terms as shall be agreed upon, between him or them and the said Isaac Allerton, our partner and agent, and deliver the same into his hands for our use; that we, the said William Bradford, William Brewster, &c. together with the said Isaac Allerton, do bind ourselves, our heirs, &c. jointly and severally, for the faithful performance of such obligations, conditions, or covenants, as shall be agreed on, &c. In witness whereof, we have put to our hands and seals, this 2d of July, Anno 1626, &c.

Upon this order, he got two hundred pounds, but it was at thirty in the hundred interest, by which appears in what straits we were; and yet this was upon better terms than the goods which were sent us the year before, being at forty-five per cent, so that it was God's marvellous providence, that we were ever able to wade through things, as will better appear if God give me life and opportunity to handle them more particularly, in another treatise more at large, as I desire and purpose (if God permit) with many other things, in a better order.

Besides the obtaining of this money, he with much ado made a composition and agreement with the body of the adventurers, Mr. Allden (something now softened by my letter before mentioned) who was one of our powerfulest opposers, did not only yield thereunto, but was a furtherer of the same. I will shew the heads of it, as it was drawn in a deed as followeth:

To all Christian people, to whom this present writing indented shall come greeting,

Whereas, at a meeting the 26th of October last past, divers and sundry persons, whose names to the one part of these presents are subscribed in a schedule hereunto annexed, adventurers to New-Plymouth, in New England in America, were contented and agreed (in consideration of the sum of one thousand and eight hundred pounds sterling, to be paid unto the said adventurers in manner and form following) to sell and make sale of all and every the stocks, shares, lands, merchandize and chatties whatsoever, to the said adventurers and other their fellow adventurers to New Plymouth aforesaid accruing or belonging, to the generality of the said adventurers aforesaid, as well by reasons of any sum or sums of money, or merchandize at any time heretofore adventured by them, or otherwise howsoever; for the better expression and setting forth of which said agreement, the parties to these presents subscribing, do for themselves severally, and as much as in them is, grant, bargain, alien, sell and transfer, all and every the said shares, goods, lands, merchandize and chatties to them belonging as aforesaid, unto Isaac Allerton, one of the planters resident at New Plymouth aforesaid, assigned and sent over as agent for the rest of the planters residing there, and unto such other planters at New Plymouth aforesaid, as the said Isaac Allerton, his heirs or assignees, at his, or their arrival shall by writing or otherwise think fit to join, or partake in the premises, their and every of their heirs and assigns in as large and ample and beneficial manner and form, to all intents and purposes, as the said several subscribing adventurers here could or may do, or perform; all which stocks, shares, lands, &c. to the said adventurers, in severalty alloted, apportioned or belonging; the said adventurers do warrant, and defend unto the said Isaac Allerton his heirs and assigns, against them, their heirs and assigns, by these presents: And therefore, the said Isaac Allerton for him, his heirs and assigns, doth covenant, promise, and grant to and with the said adventurers, whose names are hereunto subscribed, their heirs, &c. well and truly to pay, or cause to be paid unto the said adventurers or five of them, which were at the meeting aforesaid, nominated and deputed, viz. John Pocock, John Beauchamp, Robert Kean, Edward Bass, and James Shirley, their heirs, &c. to, and for the use of the generality of them, the sum of eighteen hundred pounds, of lawful money of England, at the place appointed for the receipts of money, on the west side of the Royal Exchange in London, by two hundred pounds yearly and every year, on the feast day of St. Michael, which shall be in the year 1628: And the said Isaac Allerton, for him, his heirs,. &c. doth covenant and grant to, and with the said adventurers, their heirs, &c. to do his, and their good endeavours, to procure, obtain, and get of, and from all the planters, at New Plymouth aforesaid, or so many of them as he or they by persuasion and entreaty can or may, security by several obligations, or writing obligatory, to make payment of the said sum of eighteen hundred pounds, in form aforesaid, according to the true meaning of these presents. In testimony whereof, to this part of these presents, remaining with the said Isaac Allerton, the said subscribing adventurers have set to their names, &c. And to the other part of these presents remaining with the said adventurers, the said Isaac Allerton hath subscribed his name, the 15th of November, Anno 1626, and in the second year of the reign of our sovereign Lord, King Charles, by the grace of God, King of England, &c: Subscribed thus as followeth:

John White,	Samuel Sharp,	Thomas Hudson,
John Pocock,	Robert Holland,	Thomas Andrews,
Robert Kean,	James Shirley,	Thomas Ward,
Edward Bass,	Thomas Mott,	Fria, Newbald,
William Hobson,	Thomas Fletcher,	Thomas Heath,
William Penington,	Timothy Hatherly,	Joseph Tilden,
William Quarles,	Thomas Brewer,	William Penrin,
Daniel Poynton,	John Thorned,	Eliza Knight,
Richard Andrews,	Myles Knowles,	Thomas Coventry,
Newman Rookes,	William Collier,	Robert Allden,
Henry Browning,	John Revell,	Laurence Anthony,
Richard Wright,	Peter Gudburn,	John Knight,
John Ling,	Emnu. Alltham,	Matthew Thornhill,
Thomas Goffe,	John Beauchamp,	Thomas Millsop,

This year. Anno 1627, Mr. Allerton was sent again as for other things, so especially to ratify and confirm this bargain; and for that end we gave him full authority under our hands,, and seal, and became bound in several bonds for the payment of the money yearly: So the thing was fully concluded, and the bargain fairly engrossed in parchment, under their hands and seals, as legally and formally done, as by the learnedest lawyers could be devised, as by the deed itself will better appear; which I will not here insert, being long, but the substance may be seen in the former, to which it hath reference; only I will mention this particular clause, how we were bound thereby to forfeit thirty shillings a week, for every week that we failed of due payment, at any the several days. Thus all now is become our own, as we say in the proverb, when our debts are paid. And doubtless this was a great mercy of God unto us, and a great means of our peace and better subsistence, and wholly dashed all the plots and devises of our enemies, both there and here, who daily expected our ruin, dispersion and utter subversion by the same; but their hopes were thus far prevented, though with great care and labour, we were left to struggle with the payment of the money.

A letter of Mr. Sherley's to myself upon this conclusion, as followeth:

To his very loving and much respected friend, Mr. William Bradford, Governour of Plymouth, in New-England, these.

Most Worthy and Beloved
    SIR,
I have received your letter of the 14th of June last, by your and my loving friend, Mr. Allerton, wherein it pleaseth you to express more thankfulness than I have deserved; I confess my desire is much larger than my power, to do you and those good friends with you, the good I would. We cannot but all take notice how the Lord hath been pleased to cross our proceedings and caused many disasters to befal us therein; and sure I conceive the only cause to be, we, or *many of us here, aimed at other ends than God's glory:* But now I hope that cause is taken away, the bargain being fully concluded and, as far as our powers will reach, confirmed under our hands and seals to Mr. Allerton and the rest of his and your copartners: But for my own part, I confess, as I was loath to hinder this bargain, being the first propounder thereof at our meeting, so, on the contrary side, I was as unwilling to set my hand to the sale, being the receiver of the most part of the adventures and a second causer of much of the engagements, and one more threatened, being most envied and aimed at (if

they could find any step to ground their malice on) than any other of the adventurers whosoever: I profess I know no just cause they ever had, or have so to do, neither shall it ever be proved that I have wronged them or any of the adventurers, wittingly or willingly, one penny in the disbursement of the best part of five thousand pounds, in those two years' troubles: No, the sole cause why they malice me (as I and others have conceived) was that I would not side with them against you and the going over of the Leyden; but as I then cared not, so now I little fear what they can do; yet charge and trouble I know they may cause me to be at; and for these reasons, I would gladly have persuaded the other four to have sealed to this bargain and so have left me out; but Mr. Allerton knoweth they would not; so rather than it should now fail, Mr. Allerton having taken so much pains (as I am even ;ashamed to relate) I have sealed with the rest, with this proviso and promise of Mr. Allerton's, that if any troubles arise here, you are to be at half the charge: Wherefore now I doubt not but you will give your generality good content and self peace amongst yourselves, and peace with the natives, then, no doubt but the God [4] of peace will bless your going out and returning in, and cause all that you set your hand to to prosper: The which I shall ever pray the Lord to grant, if it be his most blessed will, and that for Jesus Christ his sake.

I acknowledge myself much obliged to you, and others with you, for your good counsel and loving respect to my kinsman; I pray you continue the same still and set it as on my score to requite when occasion is offered. My wife and I most kindly remember our loves unto you and Mrs. Bradford, desiring you to remember us in your prayers, for assuredly unless the Lord be merciful unto us and the whole land in general, our estate and condition is far worse than yours; wherefore if the Lord send persecution here (which is much to be feared) and so should put into our minds to fly for refuge, I know no place safer than to come to you, for all Europe is at variance one with another, but chiefly with us) not doubting but to find such friendly entertainment as shall be honest and conscionable, notwithstanding what hath lately passed; for I profess in the word of an honest man, had it not been to procure your peace and quiet from some turbulent spirits here, I would not have sealed to this deed, though you have given me all my adventure and debt ready down: And this I leave to your serious consideration, not questioning, but you will approve yourselves faithful and honest before God and men: And thus desiring the Lord to bless, preserve and prosper you and all with you, I for this time cease, but ever resting.

Your faithful and loving friend
to my power,
JAMES SHIRLEY.

London, Dec. 27th, Anno 1627.

This year we had letters sent us from the Dutch plantation, of whom we had heard much by the natives, but never could hear from them nor meet with them before themselves thus writ to us, and after sought us out; their letters were writ in a very fair hand, the one in French, and the other in Dutch, but were one *verbatim,* so far as the tongue would bear.

[*Here follows a letter in Low Dutch, from Isaac de Razier at Manhatas, in fort, Amsterdam Mar. 9, 1627. N. S. to the Governour of New-Plymouth.*]

I will not trouble myself to translate this letter, seeing the effect of it will be understood by the answer which now follows in English, though writ to them in Dutch.

To the Honourable and Worshipful the Director and Council of New Netherlands our very loving and worthy friends and christian neighbours.

The Governour and Council of Plymouth in New England wish your Honours and Worships all happiness, and prosperity in this life, and eternal rest and glory with Christ Jesus our Lord in the world to come.

We have received your letters wherein appeareth your good will, and friendship toward us, but is expressed with over high titles, and more than belongs to us, or than is meet for us to receive: But for your good will and congratulation of our prosperity in this small beginning of our poor colony, we are much bound unto you, and with many thanks do acknowledge the same; taking it both for a great honour done unto us, and for a certain testimony of your love, and good neighbourhood. Now these are further to give your Honours, Worships and Wisdoms to understand, that it is to us no small joy, to hear, that it hath pleased God to move his Majesty's heart, not only to confirm that ancient amity, alliance, and friendship, and other contracts formerly made, and ratified by his predecessors of famous memory; but hath himself (as you say) and we likewise have been informed, strengthened the same with a new union, the better to resist the pride of that common enemy the Spaniards, from whose cruelty the Lord keep us both, and our native countries. Now for as much as this is sufficient to unite us together in love, and good neighbourhood in all our dealings; yet are many of us further tied by the good and courteous entreaty which we have found m your country; having lived there many years, with freedom and good content, as many of our friends do to this day; for which we are bound to be thankful, and our children after us and shall never forget the same but shall heartily desire your good and prosperity, as our own forever. Likewise for your friendly proposition and offer to accommodate and help us with any commodities or merchandize which you have and we want, either for beaver, otters or other wares, is to us very acceptable, and we doubt not but in short time, we may have profitable commerce and trade together: But you may please to understand that we are but one particular colony or plantation in this land, there being divers others besides, unto whom it hath pleased those Honourable Lords of his Majesty's Council for New England, to grant the like commission, and ample privileges to them (as to us) for their better profit and subsistence; namely to expulse, or make prize of any, either strangers or other English which shall attempt, either to trade, or plant within their limits (without their special licence and commission) which extends to forty degrees: Yet for our parts, we shall not go about to molest or trouble you in any thing, but continue all good neighbourhood and correspondence as far as we may; only we desire that you would forbear to trade with the natives in this bay, and river of Naragansett and Sowames, which is (as it were) at our doors: The which if you do, we think also no other English will go about any way to trouble or hinder you; which otherwise are resolved to solicit his Majesty for redress, if otherwise they cannot help themselves.

May it please you further to understand, that for this year we are fully supplied with all necessaries, both for clothing and other things; but it may so fall out, that hereafter we shall deal with you, if your rates be reasonable: And therefore when your people come again, we desire to know how you will take beaver by the pound, and otters by the skin, and how you will per cent, for other commodities, and what you can furnish us with; as likewise what commodities from us, may be acceptable with you, as tobacco, fish, corn, or other things, and what prices you will give.

Thus hoping that you will pardon and excuse us for our rude and imperfect writing in your language, and take it in good part; because, for want of use, we cannot so well express that we understand; nor happily understand every thing so fully as we should: And so we humbly pray the Lord, for his mercy's sake, that he will take both us and our native countries, into his holy protection and defence. Amen.

By the Governour and Council, your Honours' and Worships' very good friends and neighbours.

New-Plymouth, March 19th.

Next follows their reply to this our answer, very friendly but maintaining their right and liberty to trade in those parts, which we had desired they would forbear; alleging that as we had authority and commission from our king; so they had the like from the States of Holland, which they would defend.

August 7, 1627.

Another of theirs upon our answer to their last, which I here omit.

An answer to the former letters.

We have received your letters [5] dated the 7th of August, and with them a rundlet of sugar, and two Holland cheeses, by John Jacobson of Wiring; for which we give you many thanks and must remain your debtors till another time, not having any thing to send you for the present that may be acceptable: Further, you shall understand that it is also our resolution and hearty desire to hold and continue all friendship and good neighbourhood with you as far as we may and lies in our power; we desire also that we might have opportunity (according as you write) by word of mouth, to confer together touching our mutual commerce and trading in such things as our countries afford; and would now have sent one, but that one of our boats is abroad, and we have much business at home; But if by the next you would please to depute one (according as you have propounded) to come hither and to confer hereabouts, we should be glad and he should be welcome. If not, we shall send as soon as conveniently we can (after harvest) if we can know when your bark comes this way. We cannot likewise omit (out of our love and good affection toward you and the trust you repose in us) to give you warning of the danger which may befall you, that you may prevent it; for if you light either in the hands of those of Virginia or the fishing ships, which come to New England, peradventure they will make prize of you, if they can, if they find you trading within those limits; as they surprised a colony of the French, not many years since, which was seated within these bounds: For howsoever you allege in your former letter, that you have navigated and traded in these parts above this twenty-six years, and that you: company have now authority from the States and the Prince of Orange to do so; yet you must understand that her Majesty, Queen Elizabeth, of famous memory hath began to navigate and plant in these lands well nigh forty years ago, as appeareth by her patents and royal grants conferred upon divers of her subjects and since confirmed and enlarged by his late Majesty, and still continued by possession. Therefore it were best (in our opinion) that your masters should solicit the States that they might come to some order and agreement with the King's Majesty and State of England hereabout, before any inconvenience befall; for howsoever you may be assured for ourselves, yet we should be sorry to hear you should sustain harm from any of our nation; but more of these things when we shall speak one with another: In the mean time we commit you and your affairs to the protection of the highest.

Your loving friends, the Governour
and Council of New-Plymouth.
WILLIAM BRADFORD.

&c.

THEIR answer to this directed to myself thus superscribed:

Monsieur Monseignieur, William Bradford, Governeur in Nieu-Plemeuen.

This I will put in English and so will end with theirs, viz.

After the wishing of all good unto you, this serves to let you understand, that we have received your (acceptable) letters dated the 14th of the last month, by John Jacobson of Wiring, who besides, by word of mouth, hath reported unto us your kind and friendly entertainment of him: For which cause (by the good-liking and approbation of the Directors and Council) I am resolved to come myself, in friendship, to visit you, that we may by word of mouth friendly communicate of things together; as also to report unto you the good will and favour that the Honourable Lords of the authorized West-Indian company bear towards you. And to show our willingness of your good accommodation, have brought with me some cloth of three sorts and colours, and a chest of white sugar, as also some *seawan*, &c. not doubting but, if any of them may be serviceable unto you, we shall agree well enough about the prices thereof. Also John Jacobson aforesaid hath told me, that he came to you overland m six hours, but I have not gone so far this three or four years; wherefore I fear my feet will fail me, so I am constrained to entreat you to afford me the easiest means that I may, with least weariness, come to congratulate with you: So leaving other things to the report of the bearer, shall herewith end; remembering my hearty salutations to yourself and friends, &c. from a-board the bark Nassau, the 4th of October; before Frenchman's point.

Your affectionate friend.

Anno 1627.   ISAAC De RA-

ZIER.

So, according to his request, we sent our boat for him, who came honourably attended with a noise of trumpeters; he was their upper *commis,* or chief merchant and second to the Governour; a man of a fair and genteel behaviour, but soon after fell into disgrace amongst them; by reason of their factions; and thus at length we came to meet and deal together. We at this time bought sundry of their commodities, especially their *sewan* or *wampampeack,* which was the beginning of a profitable trade with us and the Indians: We further understood, that their masters were willing to have friendship with us and to supply us with sundry commodities, and offered us assistance against the French if need were. The which, though we know it was with an eye to their own profit, yet we had reason

both kindly to accept it and make use of it: So after this sundry of them came often to us, and many letters passed between us, the which I will pass by, as being about particular dealings, and would not be here very pertinent; only upon this passage we wrote one to their Lords and masters; as followeth.

Right Honourable and Worthy Lords, &c.

We understand by your agent, Mr. Isaac Razier, who is at this present with us (and hath demeaned himself to your honours and his own credit) of your honourable and respective good intentions towards us, which we humbly acknowledge with all thankfulness, and shall ever be ready in the performance of all offices of good and Christian neighbourhood, towards your colony and plantation here, and in all satisfactory correspondence to your Honours, so far as in us lieth and may stand with our allegiance to the King's most excellent Majesty, our Sovereign Lord the King of Great-Britain; acknowledging ourselves tied in a strict obligation unto your country and State, for the good entertainment and free liberty which we had, and our brethren and countrymen yet there have and do enjoy, under our most honourable Lords the States; and so shall be ready to accommodate ourselves to your good satisfaction: For the propositions of your agent concerning the matter of trade and commerce, we will have due and respective consideration, wishing it had been sooner propounded at the beginning of the year, before we sent our factor into England and Holland about our trade and supplies; for, till his return, we can determine of nothing, not yet knowing certainly what issue there will be of the business between the merchants our partners, and ourselves; and therefore desire suspension of our determination and resolution herein till the next year, we being not yet altogether free in respect of our engagements unto them: In the meantime we will digest it in our best cogitations; only we desire your Honours, that ye would take into your wise and honourable considerations, that which we conceive may be a hindrance to this accordation, and may be a means of much future evil, if it be not prevented, namely, that you clear the title of your planting in these parts, which his Majesty hath, by patent, granted to divers his nobles and subjects of quality; least it be a bone of division in these stirring evil times, which God forbid: We persuade ourselves, that now may be easily and seasonably done, which will be harder and with more difficulty obtained hereafter, and perhaps not without blows; so there may be assured peace and good correspondence on all parts, and ourselves more free and able to contract with your Honours. Thus commending our best service to our most noble Lords, praying for the prosperous success of your worthy designs, we rest your Lordships'

Most sincerely affected and bounden,

We well knew likewise, that this dealing and friendship with the Dutch (though it was wholly sought of themselves) yet it would procure us envy from others in the land, and that at one time or other, our enemies would take occasion to raise slanders and frame accusations against us for it; therefore, to prevent their malice, as also to shew the sincerity of our dealing and our loyal and dutiful respect to his Majesty and the Honourable Council for New England; we sent their first letter (with our answer thereto and their reply to the same) unto the Council as may appear more particularly by our letters following.

A letter to the Council of New England,

Right Honourable,

We held it our bounden duty to inform and acquaint your Lordships and Honours, with all such occurrences and matters of note as do here befal, and may any way concern the estate of this country, in either the good or hurt thereof, which, next his Majesty, stands under your honourable governments and protection; or which may in any sort, be worthy your wise and prudent considerations. May it please your Honours and Lordships to understand, that of late we received letters from the Dutch plantation, who using to trade near unto us, had order to stay for an answer from us; and the effect of their letters, being friendly and congratulatory, we answered them in like sort; since which time, we received another from them, but have had as yet no opportunity to give answer thereto. Their first letters were two, [6] but both one in effect and verbatim, so far as the proprieties of the tongues will bear; the French, with the copies both of our answer and their reply, we have here enclosed sent unto your Honour's view, that according to your honourable directions therein, we may govern ourselves, in our dealings with them. We further understand that for strength of men and fortification, they far exceed us, and all in this land. We cannot likewise forbear to complain unto your Lordships, of the irregular living of many in this land, who without either patent or licence, order or government, live, trade and truck, not with any intent to plant, but rather to forage the country and get what they can, whether by right or wrong, and then be gone: So as such as have been and are at great charge to settle plantations, will not be able to subsist, if some remedy be not provided, both with these and the inordinate course of fishermen, who begin to leave fishing, and fall wholly to trading, to the great detriment of both the small beginning here, and the State of England, by the unprofitable consuming of the victuals of the land upon these salvages: Whereas plantations might here better raise the same in the land, and so be enabled both to subsist and to return the profit thereof into England for other necessaries, which would be beneficial to the commonwealth. Our humble suits therefore to your good Lordships is, that you would take some such order, for redress herein, as shall seem best to your honourable wisdoms, for the relief of all the plantations in the land. So in all humbleness we commit ourselves to your honourable direction, and you to the protection of the Almighty, resting

Yours ever at commandment,

WILLIAM BRADFORD,

New-Plymouth, June 15, *Anno* 1627. *Governour,*
&c.

Another to Sir Feminando Gorges, touching the same subject.
   Honourable Sir,
   My humble duty remembered; we have of late received letters from the Dutch plantation and have had speech with some of them; I hold it my duty to acquaint your Worship and the rest of the Honourable Council therewith, unto whom we have likewise writ and sent the copies of their letters, that, together with their and your honourable directions, we may know how to order ourselves herein: They have used trading there this six or seven and twenty years, but have begun to plant of later time, and now have reduced their trade to some order, and confined it only to their company, which heretofore was spoiled by their seamen and interlopers, as ours is this year most notoriously, of whom we have made some complaint in our letters to the Council, not doubting but we shall find worshipful furtherance therein. We are now upon concluding with our adventurers, and shall be put upon hard straits by great payments, which we are enforced to make, for sundry years, or else to leave all, which will be to us very difficult; and, to say the truth, if these disorders of fishermen and interlopers, be not remedied, no plantations are able to stand, but will decay, whereas otherwise they may subsist and flourish: Thus in all humbleness I take leave, and rest.

At your service,

WILLIAM BRADFORD,

Plymouth, June 15, *Anno* 1627.
P. S. Besides the spoiling of the trade this last year, our boat and men had like to have been cut off by the Indians, after the fishermen were gone, for the wrongs which they did them, in stealing their skins and other abuses offered them, both the last year and this; and besides they still, continue

to truck pieces, powder and shot with them, which will be the overthrow of all, if it be not looked unto.

But I will now return to prosecute other letters out of England, touching our business and success thereof.

A letter of Mr. Shirley's.

To his worthy and loving friend, Mr. William Bradford, Governour of Plymouth, in New-England; these.

Thrice worthy and beloved Sir,

I have received your letter of the 26th of May, by Mr. Gibs and Mr. Goff, and with all the barrel of skins according to the contents; for which Mr. Beauchamp and I got a bill of store, and so took them up and sold them together at £78 12s. sterling, and since, Mr. Allerton hath received the money, as will appear by the account. It is true as you write, your engagements are great, not only the purchase, but you are yet necessitated to take up the stock you work upon, and that not at 6 or 8 per cent, as it is here let out, but at 30, 40, yea and some 50 per cent, which were not your gains great, and God's blessing on your honest endeavours more than ordinary, it could not be that you should long subsist, in the maintaining of and upholding of your worldly affairs: And this your honest, wise, and discreet agent, Mr. Allerton, hath seriously considered and so deeply laid to mind how to ease you of it, as I know it hath much troubled him: He told me you were contented to accept of me and some few others, to join with you in the purchase, as partners; for which I kindly thank you and all the rest and do willingly accept of it; and though absent, shall willingly and readily be at such charge as you and the rest shall think meet; and this year am contented to forbear my former £50 and two years increase for the adventure, both which now makes £80, without any bargain or condition for the profit, you (I mean the generality) standing to the adventure outward and homeward: Now (not that I would seem to boast or seek for undeserved praise) I have persuaded Mr. Andrews and Mr. Beauchamp to do the like; so as you are eased of that high rate you were at the other two years, I say we leave it freely to yourselves, allow us what you please and as God shall bless: I purpose, God willing, to be at charge of sending over a man or two; and so doth Mr. Andrews and now Mr. Beauchamp; for what course I run he desireth to do the same; and though he have been or seemed somewhat harsh heretofore, yet, now you shall find he is new moulded.

I also see, in your letter, your desire I should be your agent or factor here; truly Mr. Bradford and our worthy Governour, far be it from me to flatter you (for I profess to hate it) I have ever esteemed and found you so faithful, honest and upright men, as I have even resolved with myself (God Assisting me) to do you all the good that lieth in my power; and therefore if you please to make choice of so weak a man, both for abilities and body, to perform your business, I promise, the Lord enabling me, to do the best I can, according to those abilities he hath given me, and wherein I fail, excuse me and blame yourselves, that you made no better choice; now, because I am sickly and we are all mortal, I have advised Mr. Allerton to join Mr. Beauchamp with me in your deputation, which I conceive to be very necessary and good for you; your charge shall be no more for it is not your salary makes me undertake your business: Sir, for your love and good counsel to my kinsman, I acknowledge myself much engaged unto you, I pray you be still the same, for I know he hath much need of it.

[The rest being news, and of sundry passages about the Parliament; I omit as not pertinent to my purpose, it was concluded as followeth.]

Thus fearing I have been troublesome in relating of things, I cease, heartily desiring the long continuance of your good health to the pleasure of the Lord, and commending you and yours, and all God's faithful people wheresoever, unto the guidance and safe protection of the Almighty, ever resting

Your faithful loving friend,

JAMES SHIRLEY.

London, Nov. 17, *Anno* 1628.

Being thus deeply engaged, and a few only of us being bound to make payment of all, yea in a double bond; for besides our formal bonds, it was our credits and honesty, that made our friends rest and rely upon us, assuring themselves, that if we lived and it was possible, we would see them have their monies: Therefore we thought it our safest and best course to come to some agreement with the people, to have the whole trade consigned to us for some years; and so in the time to take upon us, to pay all the debts and set them free: Another reason which moved us to take this heavy burthen upon our shoulders was, our great desire to transport as many of our brethren of Leyden over unto us, as we could, but without this course we could never have done it, all here being (for peace and unity's sake) made joint purchasers with us, and every one thereby had as much interest as ourselves; and many were very opposite here against us in respect of the great charge: Again we well knew, that, except we followed our trading roundly, we should never be able to do the one or the other; therefore we sought means to have our patent enlarged, and to have some good trading places included therein; that if we could not keep them thereby wholly to ourselves, yet that none should exclude or thrust us wholly out of them, as we well knew that some would have done, if we now had not laid hold of the opportunity: Therefore Mr. Allerton was sent over to prosecute these things, and to acquaint those few of our friends in England, whom the year before were joined purchasers with us, what agreements we had made and concluded with our people, and for what ends, and so to offer them to be our partners in trade and the whole business; writing our letters unto them for that end.

The copy of the covenants made with the people here followeth; after the which were signed by them, we made division of the cattle and other things, every one having according to their proportion of shares, and so were set free from all engagements and debts, they resting wholly on our heads.

Articles of agreement between the Colony of Plymouth in New England of the one party; and William Bradford, Captain Miles Standish, and Isaac Allerton, and such others as they shall take as partners and undertakers with them, on the other party, made the —

First, it is agreed and covenanted betwixt the said parties, that they the said William Bradford, Captain Miles Standish, and Isaac Allerton, and such others as they shall take unto them, have undertaken, and do by these presents covenant and agree to pay, discharge and acquit the said colony, of all the debts, both due for the purchase, or any other way belonging to the same, at the day of the date of these presents.

Secondly, the above-said parties are to have and freely enjoy the pinnace, the boat at Manamett, and the shallop, called the Bass Boat, with all other implements to them belonging, that is in the store of the company; with all the whole stock of furs, fells, beads, corn, wampampeak, hatchets, knives, &c. that is now in the store, or any way due unto the same upon account.

Thirdly, that the above-said parties have the whole trade to themselves their heirs and assigns, with all the privileges thereof, as the said colony doth now, or may use the same; for six full years to begin the last of September next ensuing.

Fourthly, in further consideration of the discharge of the said debts every several purchaser, doth promise and covenant yearly to pay, or cause to be payed, to the above-said parties, during the f till term of the said six years, three bushels of com or six pounds of tobacco, at the undertaker's choice.

Fifthly, the said undertakers shall, during the aforesaid term, bestow £50 per annum in hose and shoes, to be brought over for the colony's use, to be sold them for com, at dr. per bushel.

Sixthly, that at the end of the said term of six years, the whole trade shall return to the use and benefit of the said colony, as before.

Lastly, if the aforesaid undertakers, after they have acquainted their friends in England with these covenants, do (upon the first return) resolve to perform them, and undertake to discharge the debts of the said colony according to the true meaning and intent of these presents, then they are (upon such notice given) to stand in force, otherwise all things to remain, as formerly they were, and a true account to be given to the said colony, of the disposing of all things according to the former order.

This agreement was by these subscribed; for some would not subscribe, and some were from home.

William Brewster,	Jona. Brewster,	Anthony Anable,
Cudbert Cudbers,	Stephen Trasie,	Stephen Dean,
William Palmer,	Samuel Fuller,	John Billington,
Stephen Hopkins,	Manas. Kempton,	John Shaw,
John Adams,	Edward Doty,	Wm. Wright,
Exper. Michell,	Robert Hicks,	Peter Brown,
Francis Eaton,	Thomas Prince,	William Bassett,
Phineas Pratt,	Joshua Pratt,	Francis Cook,
Edward Bangs,	John Howland,	John Fance.

The names of the undertakers, were these following, for the three before mentioned made choice of these other, and though they knew not their minds before (many of them being absent) yet they did presume they would join with them in the thing, as afterward they did.

William Bradford,	John Allden,	James Shirley,
Captain Standish,	Thomas Prince,	John Beauchamp,
Isaac Allerton,		Richard Andrews,
Edward Winslow,		Timothy Hatherly.
William Brewster,	*And these of Lon-*	
John Howland,	*don*	

This year sundry that pretended themselves to be planters, seeing the gain the fishermen made by trading of pieces, and powder, and shot to the Indians, and how they went on uncontrouled in the same, they began to practice the same: A principal head of whom was one Morton, who had gathered a profane crew unto him, and was himself an example of all wickedness unto them, who kept a house (or school rather of *Athesmy*) in the Massachusetts bay. He not only had offended in trading off sundry pieces to the Indians, but when he was by his neighbours gently admonished of the same, and shewed the evil consequences that would follow thereupon, he took it in great scorn, and said he would do it in the dispite of all; and for that end sent for many new pieces out of England; besides, as he and his consorts got much hereby, so they spent it as lewdly in maintaining drunkenness, riot and other evils amongst them; yea and inveigling of men's servants away from them, so as the mischief began to grow intolerable, and if it had been suffered a while longer would have become incurable; his neighbours about him grew afraid of him, and suffered many abuses at his hands, and knew not how to help it; but both they, and other of the weaker plantations, made suit to us, to help and assist them to take some order with him and that desperate company; we told them that we had no authority to do any thing, but seeing it tended to the utter ruin of all the whole country, we would join with them against so public a mischief; so we sent first again to admonish him, from ourselves and the rest, and signified unto him, that besides the hurt and peril he brought upon us all, his actions was flatly against a proclamation of the late King's Majesty, published to all his subjects, both in England and here, against the trucking of any pieces or other arms, to any of the Savages; his answer (after oaths and other contumelies) was, that proclamations were no law, nor enjoined no penalty; he was answered yes, the breakers incurred his Majesty's displeasure, which might prove a penalty too heavy for him to bear; he replied, that King was dead, and his displeasure died with him: Thus seeing no other remedy, at the earnest request of the other planters, and plantations in the land, we assisted and led in the apprehension of him (which was with danger enough, for he armed himself for resistance) and so, by the mutual consent of all the rest, he was sent prisoner into England, [7] to the council of New England, with letters and information against him; which letters follow:

To the Right Honourable, his Majesty's council for New England, these, Right Honourable and our very good Lords,

Necessity hath forced us, his Majesty's subjects of New England in general (after long patience) to take this course with this troublesome planter, Mr. Thomas Morton, whom we have sent unto your Honours, that you may be pleased to take that course with him, which to your honourable wisdom shall seem fit; who hath been often admonished not to trade or truck with the Indians, either pieces, powder, or shot, which yet he hath done, and duly makes provision to do, and could not be restrained, taking in high scorn (as he speaks) that any here should controul therein: Now the general weakness of us, his Majesty's subjects, the strength of the Indians, and at this time their great preparations to do some affront upon us, and the evil example which it gives unto others, and having no subordinate general government, under your Honours, in this land, to restrain such misdemeanours, causeth us to be troublesome to your Lordships, to send this party unto you for remedy and redress hereof: And not only in respect to this particular delinquent, but of the fishing ships, who make it too ordinary a practice, with whom we have neither authority nor ability to deal, and who are more encouraged when the planters themselves are so licentious herein; and therefore most humbly pray your Lordships, to

42

take into your honourable considerations that some speedy course and remedy may be taken herein; otherwise we shall be forced to quit the country, to our great grief, and dishonour to our nation; for we shall be beaten with our own arms if we abide: And that which further presseth us thus to send this party, is the fear we have of the growing of him and his consorts to that strength and height, by the access of loose persons, his house be a receptacle for such, as— we should not be able to restrain his inordinariness when we would, they living without all fear of God or common honesty; some of them abusing the Indian women most filthily, as it is notorious: And for further satisfaction of your Lordships we have sent some particular testifications which we aver upon the faith of christians to be true: And likewise this bearer, Mr. John Oldham, who can give your Honours further information upon his oath, if need so require whom we have sent with the prisoner, and to attend your Lordships pleasures: And thus most humbly beseeching your Lordships and Honours to make a favourable construction of our honest intendments herein, of our loyalty and respective service to his Majesty, and our care for the common good of this country, thus we cease, and most humbly commend your Lordships and honours to the protection of the highest.

Your Lordships most humble, &c.

June 9, *Anno* 1628.

This letter was subscribed by some of the chief of every plantation; but I have not their names to the copy, and therefore omit them; yet they may in part be seen by that which was at the same time underwritten (in another paper) towards the charge, as followeth; though it cost us a great deal more, and yet to little effect, as the event sheweth.

	£.	s.
From Plymouth,	2	10
From Naumkeak,	1	10
From Pascataquack,	2	10
From Mr. Jeffrey and Mr. Burslem,	2	
From Natascot,	1	10
From Mrs. Thomson,		15
From Mr. Blackston,		12
From Edward Hilton,	1	
-----	12	7

We wrote this following, likewise, to Sir Ferdinando Gorges.

Honourable Sir,

As you have ever been, not only a favourer, but also a most special beginner and furtherer of the good of this country, to your great cost and no less honour, we whose names are underwritten, being some of every plantation, in the land, deputed for the rest, do humbly crave your worship's help and best assistance, in the speedy (if not too late) redress of our almost desperate state and condition in this place, expecting daily to be overrun and spoiled by the Savages, who are already abundantly furnished with pieces, powder and shot, swords, rapers and *Jaflings;* all which arms and munition is this year plentifully and publickly sold unto them, by our own countrymen; who, under the pretence of fishing, come a trading amongst them; yea, one of them (as your worships may further understand by our particular informations) hath for his part sold twenty or twenty-one pieces, and one hundred weight of powder, by which you may conceive of the rest; for we hear the savages have above sixty pieces amongst them, besides other arms; in a word there is now almost nothing vendible amongst them, but such munition, so they have spoiled the trade, in all other things; and as vice is always fruitful; so from the greedy covetousness of the fishermen, and their evil example, the like hath began to grow amongst some, who pretend themselves to be planters, though indeed they intend nothing less, but to take opportunity of the time, and provide themselves and begone, and leave others to quench the fire which they have kindled; of which number Mr. Thomas Morton is one, being of late a dweller in the Massachusetts bay, and the head of a turbulent and seditious crew, which he had gathered unto him, who, dwelling in the midst of us, hath set up the like practice in these parts, and hath sold sundry pieces to the natives, who can use them with great dexterity, excelling our English therein, and have been vaunting with them, at Sowams, Narragansett and many other places, so as they are spread both north and south, all the land over, to the great peril of all our lives: In the beginning of this mischief we sought friendly to dissuade him from it; but he scorned us therein and prosecuted it the more; so as we were constrained for the safety of ourselves, our wives and innocent children, to apprehend him by force (though with some peril) and now have sent him to the council of New England to receive according to his demerits, and be disposed of as their Honours shall think fit, for the preventing of further mischief, the safety of our lives, and the terror of all other delinquents in the same kind: Now our hope and humble request is, that your worship, and those honourable of his Majesty's council for New England, will commiserate our case, tender our lives and pity our infants; and consider the great charges and expenses, that we, and our assistants and associates have been at, besides all the miseries and hardships, that we have broken through in these beginnings which have hitherto happily succeeded, for the planting of this country, which is hopeful, if it be cherished and protected against the cankered covetousness of these licentious men; if not, we must return and quit the country: Wherefore we beseech your Worship to afford us your favourable assistance and direction in bringing this man to his answer, before those whom it may concern; and to credit our true informations, sent by this bearer, lest by his audacious and coloured pretences, he deceive you, which know not things as we do; as likewise that such fishermen, may be called to account, for their great abuses offered this year and the last, as many as have been known to offend in this case; and that your worship for the time to come would be a means, in what you may that we may be strengthened with some authority, or good order amongst ourselves, for the redressing of the like abuses which may arise amongst us, till some general government be established in the land: Thus in hopeful assurance that your worship will make a favourable construction of these our honest intendments and humble requests, we commend you to the protection of the highest and rest

 June 9, *Anno* 1628.   At your service,
&c.

I now will come to the year 1629.

This year we had divers of our friends of Leyden come to us, as had long been desired, both of them and us, and by the good providence of God end the willing mindedness of our friends, was now in part effected, as will appear by this letter following.

To my worthy and well beloved friend, Mr. William Bradford, &c.

Most loving and most respected Sir, having but two days past parted from my dear and only daughter, by reason whereof nature forceth me to be full of grief and heaviness (though otherwise, I bless God, I have cause to rejoice) be entreated therefore, to accept these few lines: First I acknowledge myself much engaged unto you for your love and care over my kinsman; be entreated to enlarge my score, by the continuance thereof; and as you for your particular have occasion, make use of me, and I hope the Lord will direct my heart not to be unthankful, nor unmindful of your love. Here are now many of your friends from Leyden coming over, which though for the most part, they be but a weak company, yet herein is a good part of that end obtained which was first aimed at, and which hath been so strongly opposed by some of our former adventurers; but God hath his working in these things, which man cannot frustrate: With them also we have sent some servants, or in the ship that went lately (I think called the Talbot) and this, that these come in, is the May-flower. Now Mr. Andrews, Mr. Beauchamp, and myself, are with your love and liking, joined partners with you; the like is Mr. Collier, Mr. Thomas and Mr. Hatherly, but they no doubt will write unto you; but Mr. Andrews, and Mr. Beauchamp rely wholly on me; they are such as Mr. Hatherly could take up, for whose care and pains you and we, are much beholden unto him; we have disbursed the charges of setting them out and transporting them over, and what allowance or agreement, you and your assistants, please to make with us, we will accept of; nay if you think mete we should make them up two a piece, because our persons are absent, we will consent to what you do, and, upon your letter and answer, make good what we are too short, or what you desire herein; Mr. Hatherly hath bound them, some upon one condition and some upon another, as they could agree. I doubt not but beaver will continue a good price still, as 15 or 16 shillings per pound; it is daily more and more worn here; besides we have now peace with France, so as now much will be carried thither; and there is some likelihood for a peace with Spain, I pray God it may be for our good, which is much to be feared: Thus not being fit, to write at this time, I shall cease with my love, and my wife's, most kindly remembered to you and yours, &c.

Your loving friend to command,
JAMES SHIRLEY.

These persons were in all thirty-five, which came at this time unto us from Leyden, whose charge out of Holland into England and in England till the ship was ready, and then their transportation hither, came to a great deal of money; for besides victuals and other expenses they were all newly appareled, for there was bought for them

Of Kersey, and other cloth,	125 yards.
Of Linnen Cloth	127 ells.
Of Shoes,	66 pair.

Besides hats and other necessaries needful for them; and after their coming here, it was 16 months before they could reap any harvest, all which time they were kept at our charge which was not small: As the Lord sent these unto us, both to their and our comfort, so at the same time he sent many other godly persons into the land, as the beginning of a plentiful harvest, as will appear more fully hereafter: So as the delay of our friends was now recompensed with a large increase, to the honour of God and joy of all good men; these began to pitch at Naumkeak, since called by them Salem, to which place was come in the latter end of summer before, a worthy gentleman, Mr. John Endicott by name, and some others with him, to make some preparation for the rest; to whom (by some that came hither from thence) I had occasion to write unto him, though unknown by face, or any other way, but as I had heard of his worth, from whom I received this letter following.

To the worshipful and my right worthy friend William Bradford, *Esq. Governour of New Plymouth, these,*
Right Worthy Sir,

It is a thing not usual, that servants to one master and of the same household should be strangers; I assure you I desire it not, nay to speak more plainly, I cannot be so to you: God's people are all marked with one and the same mark, and sealed with one and the same seal, and have, for the main, one and the same heart, guided by one and the same spirit of truth; and where this is there can be no discord, nay, here must needs be sweet harmony; and the same request (with you) I make unto the Lord, that we may, as Christian brethren, be united by an heavenly and unfeigned love, bending all our hearts and forces in furthering a work beyond our strength with reverence and fear, fastening our eyes always on him that only is able to direct and prosper all our ways. I acknowledge myself much bound to you, for your kind love and care, in sending Mr. Fuller amongst us, and rejoice much that I am by him satisfied, touching your judgments, of the outward form of God's worship; it is (as far as I can yet gather) no other than is warranted by the evidence of truth, and the same which I have professed and maintained, ever since the Lord in mercy revealed himself unto me, being far differing from the common report that hath been spread of you touching that particular; but God's children must not look for less here below, and it is the great mercy of God that he strengthens them, to go through with it. I shall not need at this time to be tedious unto you, for, God willing, I purpose to see your face shortly: In the mean time I humbly take my leave of you, committing you to the Lord's blessed protection, and rest.

Your assured loving friend and servant,

JOHN ENDICOTT.

Naumkeak, May 11, *Anno* 1629.

Now shortly after the writing of this letter came these people before mentioned, and quickly grew into church order, and set themselves roundly to walk in all the ways of God, as will appear by this letter following.

To the Worshipful, his worthy, and much respected friend, Mr. Bradford, *Governour of Plymouth these,*

Most worthy and much respected friend, Mr. Bradford; I with my wife, remember our service unto you and yours, thanking you most humbly for your great kindness, when we were at Plymouth with you: Sir, I make bold to trouble you with a few lines, for to certify you, how it hath pleased God to deal with us, since you heard from us; how, notwithstanding all opposition, that hath been here and elsewhere, it hath pleased God to lay a foundation, the which I hope is agreeable to his word, in every thing: The 20th of July, it pleased God to move the heart of our Governour, to set it apart, for a solemn day of humiliation for the choice of a pastor and teacher; the former part of the day being spent in praise and teaching; the latter part was spent about the election, which was after this manner; the persons thought on (who had been ministers in England) were demanded

47

concerning their callings; they acknowledged there was a two-fold calling, the one and inward calling, when the Lord moved the heart of a man to take that calling upon him, and fitted him with gifts for the same; the second (the outward calling) was from the people, when a company of believers are joined together in covenant, to walk together in all the ways of God, every member (being men) are to have a free voice in the choice of their officers, &c. Now we being persuaded that these two were so qualified, as the apostle speaks of to Timothy, where he saith a bishop must be blameless, sober, apt to teach, &c. I think I may say as the eunuch said unto Philip, what should let him from being baptised, seeing there was water, and he believed; so these two servants of God clearing all things by their answers (and being thus fitted) we saw no reason but that we might freely give our voices for their election after this trial: Their choice was after this manner, every fit member wrote, in a note, his name whom the Lord moved him to think was fit for a pastor, and so likewise, whom they would have for teacher; so the most voice was for Mr. Skelton to be pastor, and Mr. Higginson to be teacher; and they accepting the choice, Mr. Higginson, with three or four more of the gravest members of the church, laid their hands on Mr. Skelton, using prayers therewith. This being done, then there was imposition of hands on Mr. Higginson: Then there was proceeding in election of elders and deacons, but they were only named, and laying on of hands deferred, to see if it pleased God to send us more able men over; but since Thursday, being (as I take it the 5th of August) is appointed for another solemn day of humiliation, for the full choice of elders and deacons and ordaining them; now, good Sir, I hope, that you and the rest of God's people (who are acquainted with the ways of God) with you, will say that here was a right foundation laid, and that these two blessed servants of the Lord came in at the door, and not at the window: And thus I have made bold to trouble you with these few lines, desiring you to remember us to Mr. Brewster, Mr. Smith, Mr. Fuller, and the rest of the church; so I rest, at your service in what I may till death,

CHARLES GOTT.

Salem, July 30, *Anno* 1629.

But now I will return again to Mr. Shirley's letters, and see what he saith to our last agreement.

To his worthy and approved loving friend, Mr. William Bradford, *Governour of Plymouth in New England, these,*

Most worthy Sir, and my continual loving friend

Mr. Bradford,

Your letters of the 21st of May, from Plymouth, and of the 6th of Sept. 1629 from Salem, I have received, whereby I understand of your health and welfare, and all your friends, for which great mercies and blessings, the Lord make us thankful, for answer of your loving letter and the many thanks for small courtesies, I say, in a word, I would I had power and ability to do for you and all honest men with you, according to my will and desire; but though I came short in the former, I hope the Lord will continue my love in affection, and that you will accept of what I can do: Your deputation we have received, and the goods have been taken up and sold, by your faithful agent, Mr. Allerton, myself having been in Holland near three month this summer, at Amsterdam and other places, about my affairs: I see further the agreement you have made with the generality, in which I cannot understand but you have done very well, both for them and you, and also for your friends at Leyden; Mr. Beauchamp, Mr. Andrews, Mr. Hatherly and myself, do so like it and approve of it, as we are willing to join with you in it, and, as it shall please God to direct and enable us, will be assisting and helpful to you the best that possibly we can: Nay, had you not taken this course, I do not see how you should have accomplished the end you first aimed at, and some others endeavoured these years past: We know it must keep us from the profit, which otherwise, by the blessing of God and your endeavours, might be gained; for most of those which came in May last unto you, as also these now sent, though I hope honest and good people, yet not like to be helpful to raise profit; but rather, nay certain, must, a good while, be chargeable to you and us; at which it is likely, had not this wise and discreet course been taken, many of your generality would have grudged: Again you say well in your letter (and I make no doubt but you will perform it) that now being but few on whom the burden must be, you will both manage it the better and set to it more cheerfully, having no discontents nor contradiction, but so lovingly join together in affection and counsel, as God no doubt but will bless and. prosper your honest labours and endeavours: and therefore in all respects I do not see but you have done marvellously, discreetly and advisedly, and no doubt but it gives all parties good content, I mean that are reasonable and honest men, such as make conscience in giving the best satisfaction they are able for their debt, and that regard not their own particular so much as the accomplishing of that good end for which this business was first intended.

Sir, for our business I shall refer you to our general letter, which way of advice I would entreat you to use and write a general letter, naming therein Mr. Beauchamp, Mr. Andrews, and Mr. Hatherly with myself, though, this time, they did not, nay, Mr. Hatherly would but could not write to you. Sir, I must of force break off. My wife desires to be remembered to you and yours, and I think she hath put up a small token (as a pair of stockings) for you; thus desiring the Lord to bless and prosper you, and all your, and our honest endeavours, I ever rest

Your unfeigned, and ever loving friend,
JAMES SHIRLEY.

March 8, *Anno* 1629.

P.S. Mr. Bradford, give me leave to put you in mind of one thing; here are many of your Leyden people now come over, and though I have ever had good thoughts of them, yet believe not every one, what they shall report of Mr. Allerton; he hath been a trusty honest friend to you all, either there or here: And if any do (as I know some of them are apt to speak ill of him) believe them not. Indeed they have been unreasonably chargeable, yet grudge and are not contended: Verily their indiscreet carriage here hath so abated my affection towards them, as were Mrs. Robinson well over, I would not disburse one penny for the rest.

This offence was given by some of them, which redounded to the prejudice of the whole; and indeed our friends which sent this latter company were to blame; for they now sent all the weakest and poorest, without any of note and better discretion and government amongst them, contrary to our minds and advice; for they thought, if these were got over, the other might come when they would; but partly this distaste, but especially the great charge, which both these companies came to, coming so near together, put a bar in the way; for though this company were the fewer in number, yet their charge came to an 100l more. And notwithstanding this indiscretion, yet they were such as feared God, and were to us both welcome and useful, for the most part; they were also kept at our charge eighteen months, and all new appareled and all other charges defrayed.

Another of Mr. Shirley's, *to our worthy and beloved friends Mr.* William Bradford *Governour, and the rest of our loving partners, these, at Plymouth in New England.*

Most worthy and loving friends Mr. Bradford, Mr. Brewster, Captain Standish, and Mr. Winslow, with the rest; you may marvel I join you all in one letter, having many letters from you: But Mr. Allerton may make excuse for me in this particular; it is true I have had some of your letters in July and some since by Mr. Peirce, but till our main business, the patent, was granted, I could not set my mind nor pen to writing; and Mr. Allerton was so turmoiled about it, and found so many difficulties and oppositions, as verily I would not, nay, could not, have undergone it, if I might have had a thousand pounds; but the Lord so blessed his labours (even beyond expectation in these evil days) as he obtained love and favour of great men in repute and place; he got granted from the Earl of Warwick and Sir

Ferdinando Gorges all Mr. Winslow desired in his letters to me, and more also, which I leave him to relate: Then he sued to the King to confirm their grant and to make you a Corporation, and so to enable you to make and execute laws in such large and ample manner, as the Salem or Massachusetts plantation hath it, which the King graciously granted, referring it to the Lord Keeper to give order to the solicitor to draw it up, if there were a precedent for it; so the Lord Keeper (the best of his rank) furthered it all he could, and also the solicitor; but as Festus said to Paul, with no small sum obtained I this freedom, for by the way there were many riddles which must be resolved, and many locks must be opened with the silver, nay, the golden key; then it was to come to the Lord Treasurer, to have his warrant for freeing the custom for a certain time; but he would not do it but referred it to the Council Table, and there Mr. Allerton attended, day by day, that they sat, and made great means and friends, both of Lords and secretaries, for the furtherance of it, but they were so full of other great matters, as he could not get his, or rather Mr. Bradford's petition read, and (by reason of Mr. Peirce, his being and staying with all the passengers at Bristol, even ready to set sail, and the wind good) he was forced to leave the further tending and prosecuting of it to a solicitor, and come for Bristol; but there is no fear nor doubt but it will be granted; for he hath the chief of them to friend; yet it will be marvellous needful for him to return by the first ships that come from thence, for if you had this granted, then were you complete, and might bear such sway and government, as were fit for your rank and place that God hath called you unto, and stop the mouths of base and scurrilous fellows, that are ready to question and threaten you in every action you do: And besides, if you have the custom free for seven years inward and twenty-one years outward, the charge of the patent will soon be recovered, and there is no fear of obtaining it; only such things must work by degrees, men cannot hasten it as they would; wherefore we (I write here, in the behalf of all our partners) desire you to be earnest with Mr. Allerton, and with his wife here to come, and she to spare him this one year (nay I hope but a few months more) to finish this great and weighty business, which we conceive will be much for your good and well and sure subsisting, yea, and I hope for your posterity, and for many generations to come; for I am persuaded Sir Ferdinando (how loving and friendly soever he seems to be) knows he can, nay, purposeth to overthrow, at his pleasure, all the patents he grants, but, this being obtained, he will be frustrate of his intent; and unless a Parliament should call them in (which is not likely) you need not fear, as Mr. Allerton can further certify you, and so much for this [8] costly and tedious business; now I see what most of your letters signify unto me, concerning the contracting of ourselves into a fewer number for the managing of our business and paying of our debts, which I confess are great and needful to be carefully considered of; and no doubt but we, joining in love, may soon overcome them, but we must follow it roundly and to purpose, for if we piddle out the time in our trade, others will step in and nose us; but we know and consider you have that acquaintance and experience as none the like in the. country; wherefore, loving friends and partners, be no ways discouraged with the greatness of the debt (of which I refer you to the accounts, being the only cause of my being at Bristol, and, if time permit and God enable me, shall be brought in some good and plain form) let us not fulfil the proverb, bestow twelve pence on a purse, and put sixpence in it; but as you and we have been at great charge, and undergone much for settling of you there, and to gain experience; so, as God shall please to enable us, let us make use of it and not think with 50l. a year sent you over, to raise such means as to pay our debts. [9] We see a possibility of good, if you be well supplied and fully furnished, and chiefly, if you do lovingly, and as you do (and well you do) profess to be brethren, so say as Abraham said to Lot, let there be no contention because we are brethren: I know I write to godly, wise, and understanding men, such as have learned to bear one another's infirmities and rejoice at any one's prosperity; and if I were able I would press this the more, because it is hoped by some of your and our enemies, that you will fall out amongst yourselves and so overthrow our hopeful business; nay, I have heard it credibly reported, that some have said that till you be disjointed, by discontents and factions amongst yourselves, it boots not for any to go over, in hope of getting or doing good in these parts; but we hope better things of you, and that you will not only bear with one another, and persuade, and that effectually, one another to the contrary, but that you will banish such thoughts, and not suffer them to lodge in your breasts; it is certain offences will come, but wo unto them, by whom they come, and blessed is the peace maker; which blessedness I know you all desire, and God grant you may disappoint the hopes of your foes and procure the hearty desire of yourselves and friends in this particular. I am further to acquaint you that we have sent you a large supply for your magazine, or trade, and also that we have thought good to join with one Edward Ashley (a man I think whom most of you know) but. it is only of that place whereof he hath a patent, in Mr. Beauchamp's name; and to that end have furnished him with large provisions; now if you please to be partners with us in this, we are willing you shall, for after we understood how willing and forward, Bristol men, and, as I hear, some able men of his own kindred have been, to stock and supply him, hoping of profit, we thought fit for us to lay hold of such an opportunity, and a kind of running plantation, rather than other who have not borne the burden of settling a plantation, as we have done; and he, on the other side, like an understanding young man, thought it better to join with those that had means by a plantation, to supply and back him there, rather than strangers, that look but only after profit: Indeed the Salem partners here, as Mr. Humfries, Mr. Johnson; but chiefly Mr. Cradock and Mr. Winthrop, would fain have joined with him, and, when that could not be, with us, in that business; but we not willing, and they failing they said he would strip them of all trade in those parts; and therefore they so crossed him and us in the taking of the patent, as we could not have it, but to join their name with ours in it, though Knights, and men of good rank and near the King, spake in his behalf; and this I conceive they did only to bring it to pass, that they might join with us: Now it is not known that you are partners with him, or you and we joined partners with him, but only we four, Mr. Andrews, Mr. Beauchamp, and myself and Mr. Hatherley, who desired to have the patent in consideration of our great loss we have already sustained in settling of the first plantation there; so in conclusion we agree together to take it in both our names. And now as I said before, if you please to join with us, we are willing you should partake with us in the profits, if it please God to send any: Mr. Allerton had no power, from you to make this new contract, neither was he willing to do anything therein without your consent and approbation. Mr. William Peirce is joined with us in this, and we thought it very convenient because of landing Edward Ashley and his goods there, if it please God, wind and weather serving, as I hope it will, and he will bend his course accordingly; he hath a new boat hence with him and boards to make another; and as I think four or five lusty fellows, whereof one is a carpenter: Now in case you are not willing to join in this particular with us, fearing the charge and doubting the success, yet thus much we would entreat of you to afford him all the help you can either by men, commodities or boats, yet not but that he will pay you for any thing that he hath; for I will and so desire you to keep the accounts apart, though you join with us; because there is (as you see) other partners in this, than in the other; so, for all men's wages, boats hire, or commodities which he shall have of you, make him debtor for it, and what you shall have of him, make the plantation or yourselves, debtors for it to him; and so there need be no mingling of the accounts. And now loving friends and partners, if you join in Edward Ashley's patent and business (as I cannot see but it is for your good to do) though we have laid out the money and taken up much to stock this business and the other, yet I think it conscionable and reasonable that you should bear your shares and proportion of the stock, if not by present money yet by securing us, for so much as it shall come to; for it is not barely the interest that is to be allowed, and considered of but the adventure; though I hope by the blessing of God and your honest endeavours, it may soon be payed; the years that this partnership holds is not long nor many, let all therefore lay it to heart, and make the best use of the time that possibly we can; and let every man set too his shoulder and the burden will be the lighter, for though some speak or write not of it, but are contented to do as I do, and wholly rely on me, yet I would be loath they should think themselves hardly dealt with all; but I know you are so honest and conscionable men, as you will take it into consideration and return such answer as may give good satisfaction; there is none of us would have ventured as we do, were it not to strengthen, settle, and do you good, more than our own particular profit: Mr. Fogge, Mr. Coalson, and Mr. Thomas, though they seemed earnest to be partners, yet when they saw the debt and charge fell themselves off, and left you, us, and the business; but some though honest, yet I think they minded their own particular profit so much, as both you and we may be glad we are rid of them: For Mr. Collier verily I could have wished it would have sorted with his other affairs, to have been one of us, but he could not spare money, and we thought it not reasonable to take in any partner, unless he were willing and able to spare money, and to lay down his portion of the stock; however, account of him as a sure friend, both ready and willing to do you all the offices of a firm friend. There is no possibility of doing any good in buying the debt for the purchase, I know some will not rebate the interest, and therefore let it run its course, they are to be paid yearly, and so I hope they shall according to the agreement. I have much more to write but want time, and so must be forced abruptly to break off, desiring the Lord to bless you, and us all, and all our honest endeavours, and grant that our loves and affections, may still be united and knit together in the Lord; and so we rest your ever loving friends,

JAMES SHIRLEY,
TIMOTHY HATHERLEY.

Bristol, March 19, *Anno* 1629.

    Thus it appears that our debts were now grown great about the coming over of these two companies of the Leyden people, and the large expenses about the patents, which indeed proved to be large and excessive, when we saw them: About this business of Ashley's we were forced to join in it, though we did not much like it (for the person's sake whom we feared was a knave) for if we should have furnished him with commodities and assistance, it would much have hindered our own trade; and if we should have denied this their request, we should have lost the favour of such good friends; so we thought it the safest way to join with them herein, according to their offer, though we ran a great hazard. This last company of our friends came at such a time of the year, as we were fain to keep them eighteen months at our charge ere they could reap any harvest to live upon; all which together, fell heavy upon us and made the burthen greater; that if it had not been God's mercy, it is a wonder we had not sunk under it, especially other things occurring, whereby we were greatly crossed in our supplies for trade, by which these sums should have been repaid. With this latter company of our brethren, came over many worthy and able men into the country (or rather ours with them) amongst whom was that worthy and godly gentleman, Mr. John Winthrop, Governour of the Massachusetts; and so began the plantations there, which have since much grown and increased under his godly, able, and prudent government, and the church of God, especially, to the rejoicing of our, and the hearts of all good men; of whose beginnings and proceedings something may be gathered by a letter or two of some of our own, who were then there by occasion, which follow:

A letter to myself, from Samuel Fuller, *being (at this time) in the bay of Massachusetts.*

SIR,

The gentlemen here lately come over (as I suppose you understand of their arrival ere this, by Jonathan Brewster) are resolved to sit down at the head of Charles river, and they of [10] Matapan purpose to go and plant with them. I have been at Matapan, at the request of Mr. Warham, and let some twenty of these people blood; I had conference with them, till I was weary. Mr. Warham holds that the visible church may consist of a mixed people, godly, and openly ungodly; upon which point we had all our conference, to which, I trust, the Lord will give a blessing. Here is come over, with these gentlemen, one Mr. Phillips (a Suffolk man) who hath told me in private, that if they will have him stand minister, by that calling which he received from the prelates in England, he will leave them: The Governour is a godly, wise, and humble gentleman, and very discreet, and of a fine and good temper. We have some privy enemies in the bay (but blessed be God) more friends; the Governour hath had conference with me, both in private and before sundry others; opposers there is not wanting, and Satan is busy; but if the Lord be on our side who can be against us; the Governour hath told me he hoped we will not be wanting in helping them, so that I think you will be sent for: Here is a gentleman, one Mr. Cottington, a Boston man, who told me, that Mr. Cotton's charge at Hampton was, that they should take advice of them at Plymouth, and should do nothing to offend them: Captain Endicott (my dear friend, and a friend to us all) is a second Burrow; the Lord establish him, and us all in every good way of truth: Other things I would have writ of but time prevents me; again I may be with you before this letter; remember me unto God in your prayers, and so I take my leave, with my loving salutations to yourself and all the rest.

Yours in the Lord Christ,
SAMUEL FULLER.

Massachusetts, June 28, Anno 1630.

To our loving brethren and Christian friends Mr. William Bradford, *Mr.* Ralph Smith, *and Mr.* William Brewster, *these be.*

    Beloved, &c.

Being at Salem the 25th of July, being the Sabbath, after the evening exercise Mr. Johnson having received a letter from the Governour, Mr. Winthrop, manifesting the hand of God to be upon them, and against them, at Charlestown, in visiting them with sickness and taking divers from amongst them, not sparing the righteous, but partaking with the wicked in those bodily judgments, it was therefore by his desire, taken into the godly consideration of the best here, what was to be done to pacify the Lord's wrath; and they would do nothing without our advice, I mean those members of our church, there known unto them, viz. Mr. Fuller Mr. Allerton and myself, requiring our voices, as their own, when it was concluded, that the Lord was to be sought in righteousness; and so to that end the sixth day (being Friday) of this present week is set apart, that they may humble themselves before God, and seek him in his ordinances; and that then also such godly persons that are amongst them and known each to other, publicly at the end of their exercise, make known their godly desire, and practice the same, viz. solemnly to enter into covenant with the Lord to walk in his ways; and since they are so disposed of in their outward estates, as to live in three distinct places, each having men of ability amongst them, there to observe the day, and become three distinct bodies; not then intending rashly to proceed to the choice of officers, or the admitting of any other into their society than a few, to wit, such as are well known unto them, promising after to receive in such, by confession, as shall appear to be fitly qualified for that estate; and, as they desired to advise with us, so do they earnestly entreat that the church at Plymouth would set apart the same day, for the same ends, beseeching God as to withdraw his hand of correction, so to establish and direct them in his ways; and though the time be very short, yet since the causes are so urgent, we pray you be provoked to this godly work, wherein God will be honoured, and they and we undoubtedly have sweet comfort in so doing: Be you all kindly saluted in the Lord, together with the rest of our brethren: The Lord be with you and his spirit direct you, in this and all other actions that concern his glory and the good of his:

    Your brethren in the faith of Christ,

And fellowship of the gospel,
Salem July 26, *Anno* 1630.   SAMUEL FULLER, EDWARD WINS-
LOW.

To his loving friend, Mr. William Bradford, *Governour of Plymouth, these.*

SIR,

There is come hither a ship (with cattle, and more passengers) on Saturday last; which brings this news out of England; that the plague is sore, both in the city and country, and that the University of Cambridge is shut up by reason thereof; also, that there is like to be a great dearth in the land by reason of a dry season. The Earl of Pembroke is dead, and Bishop Laud is Chancellor of Oxford; and that five sundry ministers are to appear before the High Commission, amongst whom, Mr. Cotton, of Boston, is one. The sad news here is, that many are sick, and many are dead, the Lord in mercy look upon them! Some are here entered into a church covenant, the first four, namely, the Governour, Mr. John Winthrop, Mr. Johnson, Mr. Dudley, and Mr. Willson; since that, five more are joined unto them, and others it is like will add themselves to them daily. The Lord increase them, both in number and holiness, for his mercy's sake. I here but lose time and long to be at home, I can do them no good, for I want drugs, and things fitting to work with: I purpose to be at home this week (if God permit) and Mr. Johnson, and Captain Endicott will come with me; and upon their offer, I requested the Governour to bear them company, who is desirous to come, but saith he cannot be absent two hours. Mrs. Cottington is dead. Here are divers honest Christians that are desirous to see us; some out of love, which they bear to us, and the good persuasion they have of us; others to see whether we be so evil, as they have heard of us. We have a name of love and holiness to God and his saints; the Lord make us answerable and that it may be more than a name, or else it will do us no good. Be you lovingly saluted, and my sisters, with Mr. Brewster, and Mr. Smith, and all the rest of our friends. The Lord Jesus bless us and the whole Israel of God.   Amen.

Your loving brother in law,
Charlestown, August 2, Anno 1630.   SAMUEL FULLER.

But this worthy gentleman, Mr. Johnson, was prevented of his journey, for shortly after he fell sick and died, whose loss was great and much bewailed.

Notes

[1] Pullen, an obsolete word for poultry.
[2] This was unquestionably a misreading and should have been "Ouldom", *i.e.* "Oldham."— Editor.
[3] These letters I have not.
[4] He hath hitherto done it, blessed be His name!
[5] This was wrote in their own tongue.
[6] The one in French and the other in Dutch.
[7] And his consorts were dispersed.
[8] It was costly indeed, in the conclusion.
[9] Here the sum of the debts and other things were blotted out again.
[10] Since called Dorchester.